THE INVESTORS' HANDBOOK

THE INVESTORS' HANDBOOK

PROSHARE'S NO-NONSENSE GUIDE TO SENSIBLE INVESTING

Maggie Drummond

PROSHARE

B. T. BATSFORD LTD · LONDON

Batsford Business Online: www.batsford.com

First published 1994
This edition 1998

Published by B T Batsford Ltd,
583 Fulham Road,
London SW6 5BY

Batsford Business Online: www.batsford.com

Printed by
Redwood Books
Trowbridge
Wiltshire

ISBN 0 7134 8481 0

A CIP catalogue record for this book
is available from The British Library

CONTENTS

INTRODUCTION

The stockmarket can be baffling. It has its own language, its own way of judging and reacting to economic news and trends, its own fads and fashions for particular shares, industries and business personalities. All this gives it a mystique that intrigues as well as bewilders potential investors who would love to get involved in the stockmarket if only they understood more about it. If you are one of them then ProShare's ***The Investors' Handbook*** is for you.

You may be one of the millions of investors who became shareholders for the first time by applying for shares in British Gas, British Telecom or other privatisations. Maybe you have received 'windfall' shares from your building society when it floated on the stockmarket and want to know more about how it all works. Even if you don't hold shares directly, the chances are that your financial future is nonetheless closely linked to what happens on the stockmarket.

Unit trusts, for example, have long been popular with investors. If you have a personal or company pension scheme or a savings plan or an endowment policy with an insurance company you will, one way or another, have your investments tied up in the stockmarket.

These are all collective forms of investment where professional managers decide which shares or other investments to buy or sell. But the private investor is still faced with a baffling array of choices.

So there is no substitute for having a good working knowledge of the stockmarket when it comes to seeing your way through the sales patter and deciding what kind of investments will be best for you.

The incentives to save for the future have never been stronger. Investment in the stockmarket should be a crucial element in an individual's long-term financial planning. But it is probably the least well understood.

The Investors' Handbook takes you step by step through the maze. It aims to answer all your questions – plus some you may not have yet thought of. It tells you what you need to know about the stockmarket and how to make the best of it.

When you have read this book you will have the basic knowledge you need to set about stockmarket investment. You won't always get it right – no one does – not even the professionals. But if you apply your common sense and judgement and keep your personal objectives firmly in mind, you are likely to succeed. You will find the stockmarket fascinating – developing a real interest in events will be a crucial element in your success.

We hope this book helps you enjoy investing.

And good luck.

Wealth Warning

The information contained in this book is intended as a guide only and does not constitute investment advice. ProShare does not accept liability for any of the decisions taken as a result of using this guide. Remember that the value of shares can go down as well as up.

ONE

WHAT ARE SHARES AND WHY INVEST IN THEM?

What is a share?

A share in a company is just that. Buying shares in High Tech Enterprises plc (HTE plc) makes you a part owner for as long as you have them. Originally, our mythical company would have been privately owned, probably by the entrepreneur who started the business. In order to raise capital for expansion, HTE plc shares are offered to investors through the Stock Exchange, essentially a market, where they can be bought and sold at a price that reflects supply and demand.

Why buy them?

Whether you buy them through a new issue like a privatisation, have received them from your building society or acquire them in the 'second-hand' (or secondary) market which is the main business of the Stock Exchange, the reasons for investing in the shares are the same. You believe HTE plc is a company that is going to prosper in the future. Its profits are going to grow over the years. The dividend payments it makes to shareholders out of its profits each year are going to rise, so you look forward to an increasing income.

You also expect the share price to rise – reflecting the profits and dividend growth which should make the company, of which you are a part owner, more valuable. Buying shares is the most direct way of investing in the long-term success of a business – or, indeed, of the economy.

Shares are risk capital

Companies can raise money in a number of ways. They can go to the bank and ask for a loan. The bank will receive interest, take a charge on some of the company's assets as security and expect the loan to be repaid at the end of the agreed period. The bank does not get any direct benefit from the growth of the business. If profits fall, it does not affect its return. If the company fails, the bank, along with other creditors, has a claim on the assets. However, shareholders are last in the queue.

They will only receive some payment if the company has assets left after all other creditors have been paid.

Shareholders' returns are not guaranteed. Company profits can fluctuate – so can the dividends which are paid out of those profits. Most companies will try to maintain their dividend payments even in a recession. But a large fall in profits will usually mean a reduced dividend and a lower return for shareholders.

Share prices fluctuate as well – often in a way that baffles shareholders. There are almost as many theories as to why shares go up and down as there are shares – but here are some of the reasons:

- Good or bad news from the company
- The expectation of good or bad news from the company
- Take-over rumours
- Change of management
- Economic news and other external influences.

We will discuss the impact of these and other factors in more detail in later chapters as well as the effect of economic trends on shares prices. Anticipating share price and market movements is one of the key elements of successful stockmarket investment, so getting your timing right is very important.

Shares are different from other more familiar types of investments.

While there are risks with shares, the potential for reward is higher. As an example, let us take the standard building society investment – one of the most popular ways to save money. You receive interest on your savings and the money is safe and easily accessible. Building society savings are and should be an important part of your financial planning – but not all of it.

What is happening to the value of your capital?

When interest rates are high, as they were in the early 1990s, the return on bank and building society deposits may keep pace with inflation – or perhaps even better it. But when interest rates are low, you run the risk of the real value of your savings being eroded. There is little chance of your original capital growing to keep abreast of, or better, inflation.

While you can receive a good income from shares (we will discuss this later), one of their main attractions is providing a hedge against inflation. As the chart on page 15 shows, over the long-term, investment in the stockmarket has proved one of the best ways of maintaining the real value of your capital – and of increasing it. Which is why it has a crucial part to play in your financial planning.

There are of course different kinds of strategies involved in stockmarket investment – and how you approach it depends on:

- the amount you want to invest;
- the time you are prepared to devote to it.

You might want to invest in 'Blue Chip' companies – substantial corporations which are often household names – where a steady growth in dividends is the order of the day. You might want to find exciting 'high growth' companies, pin-point good recovery prospects, or speculate in 'penny' shares.

We will deal with all these in later chapters and so help you decide what kind of share portfolio you should have. But first, you have to look at your own financial position and decide how much of your money you should invest in the stockmarket.

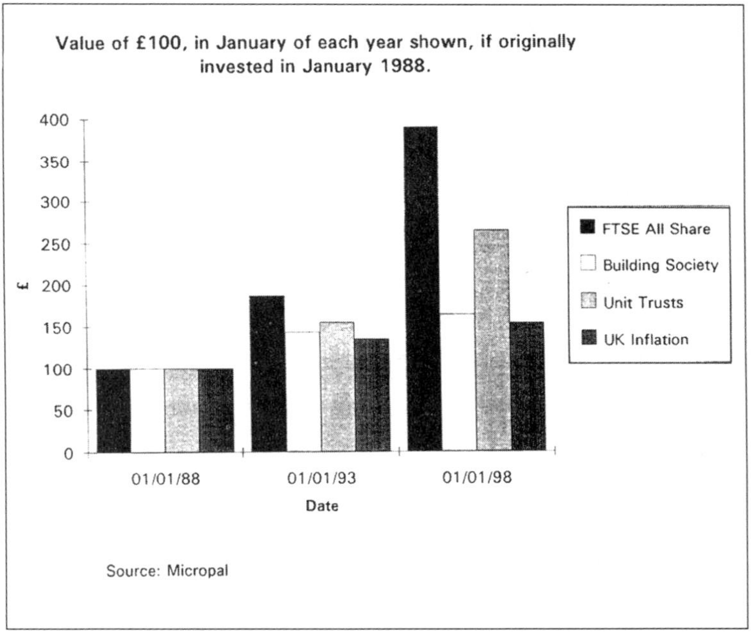

Value of £100, in January of each year shown, if originally invested in January 1988.

Source: Micropal

TWO

BEFORE YOU START

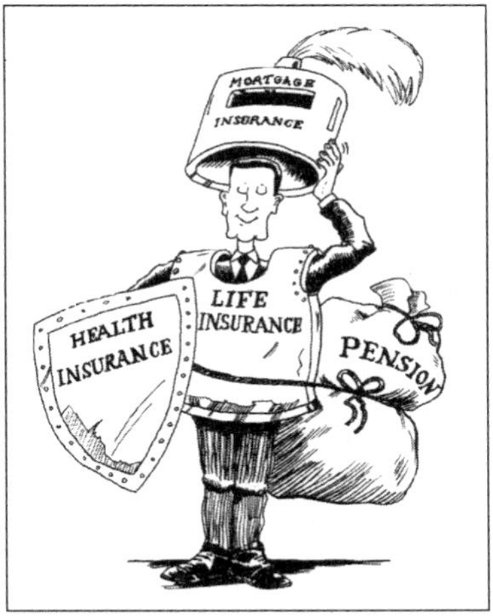

Insurance

If you have a job, a mortgage and a family, the most basic first step in financial planning is to make sure you have adequate insurance. That means life assurance, mortgage insurance – maybe permanent health insurance as well. What would happen to your family if you were unable to work or you died?

Pension

If you are in a company pension scheme, you may wish to check your entitlements. If you have moved jobs several times, your prospective pension may not look too wonderful. Take advantage of the full tax relief available to top up your pension – either by paying more into the company scheme by way of additional voluntary contributions (AVCs), or by investing in one of the many individual AVC schemes available from insurance companies.

If you do not have a company pension or if you are self-employed, you should put some money into a personal pension plan.

Short term cash

You should build up a fund of spare cash – money that you can put aside to earn a good return, perhaps in a bank or building society – somewhere you can gain immediate access in a crisis.

What are you investing for?

No-one should have all their capital invested in shares – particularly if you are saving for specific items such as school fees, where you are committed to spending at a certain point. Needless to say, buying shares is not the most appropriate way to save for a holiday, a deposit on a house, or a new car. What if your shares have fallen in value when you need the cash? A share portfolio should be a long-term investment. If you rely on your investments to produce a sizeable proportion of your income, you will need a high and predictable return from part of your portfolio – from gilts (government stocks), or guaranteed-income bonds for instance – or from higher-yielding shares.

Long-term goals

Once you have decided on your immediate financial priorities, you can think about buying shares. The essence of share investment is to enable your capital to grow over the years.

For some people, the biggest concern is having enough money to retire on comfortably – maybe retire early (this may not be voluntary these days), change careers, or just go fishing. Others want to leave a nest egg for their children. To do all of these you need to make your money work for you.

In the next chapter, we take a closer look at the kind of shares you should be investing in and learn more about the workings of the stockmarket.

THREE

TYPES OF SHARES, USEFUL JARGON AND TWO KEY MEASUREMENTS

There are approximately 3,000 companies with shares quoted on the London Stock Exchange. Some are billion pound conglomerates, others are valued at just a few million pounds. They represent the whole range of economic activity. Look at the daily list of share prices in the financial press. There you will find them divided into different sectors – motors, food retailers, chemicals, oils, property, and so on. But how do you set about choosing which areas are for you?

Spreading the risk

One fundamental rule of investment is to spread your risks – don't put all your eggs in one basket. That means building a balanced portfolio with holdings in several different companies and industries. If one sector or company has a particularly bad time, you'll have your other shares to see you through. This doesn't mean, however, you have to stick only to big safe companies (they can have bad times, too). There should be some room for a bit of exciting speculation in your portfolio – it's fun and that's where you can make some real gains – or suffer some losses! But it's important to balance your wilder hunches with solid shares. You should work out what proportion of your money you should invest where.

Knowing your shares

Unfortunately, shares do not come ready labelled 'low risk', 'high risk', 'sure-fire winner', or 'good old dependable'. But the stockmarket recognises different kinds of shares – not just by size or industrial activity – as having particular characteristics. To build your portfolio you should get to know them.

Blue Chip companies

These are big established companies – many of them are household names like Marks and Spencer, Unilever, ICI, BT and Shell. They are the 'first division' in financial terms with solid track records of substantial profits and dividends. They are large, valued by the stockmarket at over £5 billion, and form the backbone of the giant portfolios run by pension funds and insurance companies which need to invest in large quantities of shares. A lot is known about these companies – teams of stockbrokers' analysts spend their days researching them and producing regular reports.

As a result, their share prices tend to be more stable than smaller companies, although there can be exceptions. Because of their size, they reflect the general movement of the economy, the stockmarket and of their particular sectors. They are a sensible foundation for any portfolio. Although they are new to the stockmarket, the building societies that have turned themselves into banks and given windfall shares to their customers rank as Blue Chips because of the size and quality of their businesses.

Growth companies

Spotting one of these in its infancy – before it is generally recognised as something special – is every investor's dream. Typically, a growth company will be in an expanding sector of the economy where a go-ahead management has produced higher-than-average profits growth for several years in a row. It may have unique product or a technical edge. Anyone who bought Body Shop as a new issue, or in its earlier years, for instance, will have seen a handsome return. Pharmaceuticals company Glaxo Wellcome is another example.

These growth companies command a stockmarket premium – the dividend yield is lower and the price/earnings ratio is higher (see pages 27-29) because investors are buying the prospect of fast-growing profits and dividends for the foreseeable future. But a 'glamour rating' is vulnerable if growth slows, as it invariably does eventually. Investors need to be alert.

Recovery shares

Most companies reflect the general trend of the economy – but some shares really magnify the ups and downs. When times are tough, profits of some companies fall by more than average, but when things get better they can improve enormously. There are good profits to be made from these shares if you get the timing right. Industries like house-building, car components, electronics and furniture retailing are where you will find plenty of recovery candidates, particularly when the economy is coming out of recession – but check that the company is basically sound. Individual companies that have fallen on hard times for one reason or another can be good recovery prospects, too. Look out for a change in management, for example.

High-income shares

Many consider high-income shares less risky than the glamorous growth shares, because when the opportunities for profits growth are poor, a good dividend yield means investors still get a decent return. High-income shares can give a good capital performance when the stockmarket rises as well, but you should choose carefully. A high yield can also be a distress signal – particularly one that is nearing double figures. It could well mean the shares are anticipating falling profits and a reduced dividend instead. You could be looking at a recovery share – or a company heading for the corporate graveyard.

Penny shares

These are fun, offering you more shares for your money which makes you feel good. But be warned – they are a gamble.

A penny share only has to move by a few pence to produce a very large percentage rise – that's the great attraction – or fall, and that's the great risk. One drawback is that penny share 'spreads' – the difference between the current buying and selling prices – can be disproportionately large. Some penny shares are companies where profits have fallen and might recover. Others may be 'shells' where the business is stagnant. They are a target for entrepreneurs who see them as a backdoor way of getting a stockmarket quotation for their own business. Anything can happen, and frequently does.

Alternative Investment Market

Alternative Investment Market (AIM) shares have proved very popular with private investors since the Stock Exchange created this entrepreneurial market. The idea was to give new companies the chance to raise money without having to show a track record and conform with all the stringent regulations of the main stockmarket. In a very real way, the creation of the AIM fulfils one of the main historical functions of the stockmarket – raising capital for new business ventures.

It is important to recognise that many of these companies are speculative, but the AIM includes exciting companies developing new processes and techniques in biotechnology, health and other research-orientated fields, as well as conventional businesses. But investors must be wary of some of the grandiose prospects held out by these companies and be prepared to do some serious research of their own. The ranks of the AIM include some big winners and some big losers.

Useful share jargon

Shares are sometimes described as defensive. This has nothing to do with jet fighters or tanks. It means that certain industries are less affected by downswings in the economy. Major food retailing companies for example may be considered defensive – we all have to eat.

Cyclical shares are the reverse of defensive. These are companies whose business and profits are very sensitive to economic trends – see recovery shares.

High-gearing sounds painful and can be. Highly-geared companies have large borrowings by comparison with their share capital. When interest rates rise, the increased cost of those borrowings can make a big dent in profits, magnifying the effect of any slowdown in the company's actual trading results.

The term 'highly rated' can apply to a whole share sector where future prospects are considered to be particularly good, or to an individual company. The stockmarket puts a high value on these companies compared with the average.

Why not pick some individual shares for a hypothetical portfolio? Keep track of them for a few weeks. Watch how they respond to economic news, company news and the general trend of the stockmarket.

Later in this book we will take a detailed look at analysing individual companies. But you can't start to look at shares without understanding the two main yardsticks by which the stockmarket evaluates them.

Dividend yield

A dividend is the amount of income paid per share each year to investors.

The dividend yield is the return from the income, expressed as a percentage of the money you paid for the share. In practice, it is complicated to work out. Dividends are paid by companies with basic-rate tax already deducted, but the yield is worked out on the gross amount – before tax is taken off. We will deal with the personal tax aspects of owning shares later. For the moment, you can look at the share tables in the financial press. Most show the dividend yield of each share listed. What are those yields telling us?

- A very high yield may be a sign that the company is expected to cut its dividend. The share price has already fallen in anticipation of reduced profits, but the yield is reflecting last year's pay out and not the lower amount that was expected.

- A low yield often indicates that a company's profits, and therefore dividends, are expected to grow faster than average. The share price has risen in anticipation of this rising income.

- Relative yields are a useful way of comparing shares. A company whose shares are yielding lower than the sector average may grow faster than one that is yielding higher than average.

Yields on shares are the stockmarket equivalent of the rate of interest paid by other kinds of investments. Because the stockmarket offers the prospect of capital growth as well as an annual return, average dividend yields are lower than, say, the return from a building society, where the amount of the capital goes neither up, nor down.

Price/earnings ratio

The price earnings ratio is the stockmarket's other main tool for comparing one share with another. It tells you how many years it would take for the net profit after tax (known as earnings) attributable to each share of the company to equal the current share price. We will explain earnings in more detail later. Assuming a company makes 10p a share earnings, and the share price is 100p, then the price/earnings ratio is 10 (100p dividend by 10p of earnings).

The price/earnings ratio is often simply called the 'p/e' ratio. Sometimes people use the expression 'so many times earnings', or 'so many years' earnings'. They all mean the same thing.

Many newspapers publish price/earnings ratios in their share price lists. Once again, they can be misleading because they are calculated on last year's historic profits. Like dividends, they tell us different things.

- A high price/earnings ratio generally means that the company is expected to grow quickly, and increase earnings rapidly.

- A low price/earnings ratio effectively indicates that the company is rated a plodder, or one where profits might fall.

- Like relative yields, relative p/e ratios are a useful way of comparing shares. A company whose shares have a lower p/e ratio than the sector average may grow faster than one that has a p/e that is higher than average.

You might hear the stockmarket pros talking about a ‘prospective’ or a ‘forecast’ p/e ratio. This means that the calculation has been made on the basis of earnings that the company is expected to produce in the current year or in the future.

Unlike dividend yields, price/earnings ratios cannot be compared with returns on other forms of investment.

FOUR

BUYING AND SELLING SHARES

Many investors had their first taste of the stockmarket through a privatisation or a new issue – the sale of shares in a company 'floating' on the market. You fill in the application form, send off the cheque and, if you are lucky, get the shares you want. Many other investors have received shares for the first time through the demutualisation of their building societies. Easy. But then what?

When it comes to buying more shares – or selling the ones you've got – many new investors are uncertain what to do next. You may want to back your own judgement from the start. You may want advice. Or you may want to find someone who will manage your financial affairs for you. Don't be put off by fears that no one is interested in the small investor. Many firms are, but to get the kind of service you want, you have to do a bit of research.

Where do you start?

To buy and sell shares you need to use the services of a stockbroker. Today, many high street banks and building societies provide stockbroking services, so it is a good idea to shop around and speak to a number of brokers about their services and charges before you make a decision.

It is important to understand that one stockbroker can be very different from another when it comes to the services they offer. Nowadays, a stockbroking firm may be part of a huge financial conglomerate in the City. Or it may be an independent company specialising in private clients.

There are many good stockbrokers outside the City. Before you approach a stockbroker, you should find out what kind of firm it is. A free directory of private client stockbrokers is issued by the Association of Private Client Investment Managers and Stockbrokers (112 Middlesex Street, London EI 7HY), which makes choosing a suitable stockbroker much easier for you.

Banks have been keen to advertise their services to small shareholders in recent years – you can now go into some branches and buy shares at the touch of a button. Many banks own stockbroking companies. Even if yours does not, it should be able to buy and sell shares through a stockbroker on your behalf.

Some building societies offer share dealing services. If you were lucky enough to have received windfall shares, you should have been sent information on share ownership.

You can buy and sell shares through independent financial advisers (IFAs), too. They will not be members of the London Stock Exchange, but they will place your orders with a London Stock Exchange member firm.

What kind of service do you need?

The Association of Private Client Investment Managers and Stockbrokers (APCIMS) Directory explains the range of services available. But before you choose a firm you have to decide what kind of service you want.

Dealing or execution only

This is the most basic buying and dealing share service for those who don't need advice or help with financial planning. Many private client stockbrokers offer this kind of low-cost service, taking orders by telephone or post. Some stockbrokers have developed on-line services that enable clients to place orders electronically through their personal computers.

Most banks, some building societies and specialist telephone services offer an execution-only service. If you are very confident of your own judgement – or only want to buy and sell shares very occasionally – an execution-only service could be the cheapest option.

But it should be stressed that there is no personal contact – and investors are on their own when it comes to decision-making. Nonetheless, execution-only brokers have developed a wide range of services for investors that include useful information on both individual shares and the stockmarket in general. More active investors may find it worthwhile to select a service which charges a joining fee or annual charge but where the minimum commissions on each deal are low. If an execution-only stockbroker sounds right for you there is a whole variety of different services on offer depending on how active an investor you want to be, so it is worth shopping around.

Advisory

But if you want someone to talk to and advise you on stockmarket investment, you will find that most stockbrokers offer an advisory service (dealing with advice) for private clients who want to take the final decisions themselves. This is the traditional stockbroking service. If you want to take an active interest in share investment without going it alone, this might appeal to you. You may pay a little more (minimum commissions per deal may be higher for instance) but it gives you access to the firm's own research and investment ideas – and you get a sounding board for your own ideas. The stockbroker will phone you with investment suggestions.

An advisory service is non-discretionary. This means that the final decisions are always left up to you. Nothing will be bought or sold without your say so.

There are different kinds of advisory services ranging from purely reactive services where a stockbroker only responds to your requests for advice on specific shares, to more proactive services where your stockbroker keeps tabs on your whole portfolio as well providing other services, such as regular valuations, for instance. Some stockbrokers stipulate a minimum size of investment before they take on a client. Others may want to establish how active an investor you are likely to be. When it comes to choosing a stockbroker, there is absolutely no substitute for meeting the person who will be dealing with your account face to face and making sure that you both know what your personal investment objectives are. It's important that you feel comfortable talking to the person who will be your main contact. There are plenty of stockbrokers specialising in private client business. There may be several based locally and that's maybe a good starting point. You may get a recommendation from a friend who is already a client. Finding the right stockbroker is as important as comparing costs.

Portfolio management

Stockbrokers and independent financial advisers offer portfolio management services to private clients who prefer to hand over the prime responsibility for their investment decisions to professionals. Portfolio management is usually offered as a discretionary service. This means that once your investment objectives have been established, shares will be bought or sold on your behalf without you being consulted first, but you will be informed after each and every deal.

You may need to have a certain size portfolio before a stockbroker will take you on – some firms stipulate a minimum of £100,000 – others may try and steer clients with less than, say £50,000, into unit trusts instead of shares. But, as the APCIMS Directory shows, there are plenty of stockbrokers requiring far less than that – or no minimum at all. A portfolio management service could include annual valuations, advice on tax planning, regular stockmarket information, administrative paperwork and safekeeping of share certificates. The cost of these may be covered by an annual charge or by separate fees for each service you want.

Whatever service you opt for, make sure you understand the basis of charging and are absolutely clear whether it's discretionary or non-discretionary.

How much does it cost?

In the main, stockbrokers make their living on the commission paid by clients when they buy and sell shares. Each firm will have its own rates based on the size of the bargain – the value of the shares bought and sold. There are no fixed rates, costs vary from firm to firm, and there will probably be a minimum charge for small deals. Intermediaries are entitled to add their own charge if they deal with a stockbroker on your behalf.

Many stockbrokers still charge between $^1/_2$% and 2% to purchase or sell shares of up to £5,000 in value, for instance, but will reduce the percentage commission on a sliding scale for larger amounts. Smaller purchases or sales, or bargains as they are known, may have a minimum charge. This could be between £10 and £35 or more. A larger minimum charge may suggest the stockbroker is not really interested in small investors – a lower minimum indicates the firm is keen and probably specialises in low cost services for private investors.

Other share dealing charges are $^{1}/_{2}$% stamp duty (on purchase only) and sometimes a compliance charge (which helps pay for the regulator). Once the deal is done, you will receive a contract note which you should keep carefully.

Paying for shares

Most stockmarket transactions are settled five days after shares have been bought or sold. If you are sending a cheque by post, that can pose problems and there may be a penalty if the stockbroker receives payment late. Many stockbrokers accept payment by debit card over the phone. Alternatively, you may set up an account with the firm so that money is already there to meet the cost of share purchases. Some stockbrokers will still give you ten days to pay following a transaction.

The London Stock Exchange system of settlement has recently undergone important changes. In the past the transfer and administration of share ownership involved a blizzard of paperwork for everyone. Now stockmarket transactions are done through an electronic system known as Crest which registers transfers.

As a result of these changes, many investors find it more convenient to hold their shares through nominee accounts organised by their broker. If you hold your shares through a nominee account, you are still the 'beneficial' owner of the shares and receive dividends, but you do not receive share certificates and your name will not appear on the share register of the company you have invested in. Many investors find nominee accounts very convenient because their broker takes care of most of the paperwork. If you hold your shares through a nominee account you will not automatically get the company's annual reports, or invitations to its annual meeting where you have the right to vote, and you might lose your entitlement to shareholders' perks that may be offered by the companies you invest in.

However, in many cases, your broker will be able to arrange for you to participate fully as a shareholder and receive annual reports and other correspondence. Check first to see if the broker makes any charge for these additional services.

ProShare has devised a voluntary code of practice, the *ProShare Nominee Code*, to which brokers and companies can sign up. Those brokers who keep to the code are required to make their charges known fully, provide clear information about how investments held in their nominees are protected and to make arrangements, if asked, for the underlying investors to receive copies of annual reports and accounts of the companies whose shares are held.

You can choose the traditional route and have your share certificates and be registered in your own name as a shareholder in the company, although it may involve an extra charge. You have to keep your paperwork carefully.

There is another option. Active stockmarket investors can become sponsored members of Crest. As a sponsored member of Crest, your shares will be held electronically, cutting out much of the paperwork, but you keep all the rights of registered shareholders. There is an annual fee of £20 – but some stockbrokers may offer sponsored membership free. Further details about Crest and nominee accounts can be found in ProShare's *Investor Update* number 8 'What is a nominee?' and number 10 'What is CREST?'. Details of how to obtain these free fact sheets are contained in Chapter Seventeen.

The way in which you are going to hold your shares is one of the things you must agree with whatever stockbroking firm you choose.

The commission charge is not the only thing to look at when deciding who to deal with. A good broker may get you a better price, which can more than make up for his higher charges. Some brokers cut charges because they do not carry out your order at once – and you may suffer for that delay.

If you opt for dealing with advice, try to find out just how much attention you are going to get – a small country firm may be a better deal for the modest investor than a City one with lots of large clients and heavy overheads to cover.

Make sure you know the basis for charging right from the start – whether there is an annual charge for example.

Even if you opt for the discretionary portfolio, keep an eye on what is going on. Make sure you are not being traded in and out frequently (known as 'churning') and paying lots of commission to the broker, without much profit to you.

Your stockbroker may also be what is known as a market maker, meaning that they deal with shares on their own account and determine the price for that share according to supply and demand. A market maker should tell you when you are dealing in a share where his firm makes the market. That means he may be selling you shares his firm owns, or buying shares his firm wants itself. In some cases, this will mean you actually get a better deal. It should never mean that you get sold shares his firm wants to get rid of.

Beware of independent financial advisers who ring regularly with suggestions of shares for you to buy. They may have bought a lot of them cheaply, and be trying to sell them on to you at a higher price.

FIVE

WHAT MAKES SHARE PRICES MOVE?

Whether you are sizing up an individual share or looking at the market as a whole, it's most important to grasp one fundamental point: Successful stockmarket investment is about anticipation – assessing what is going to happen in six months, a year or even 18 months from now. Understanding that is as important as keeping an eye on what is happening at the moment. This is one of the things that baffles people about the stockmarket. When a company announces a big profits upturn it is often greeted with indifference by the stockmarket – the share price may even fall. This is because the profits increase was

anticipated – the shares had already risen – to use the jargon, the upturn was already 'in the price'. The market had already discounted the good results.

The professionals, the share analysts and fund managers, will already be looking a year ahead. Is the company going to produce another spectacular rise in profits? Will there be a slowdown in growth? Or, even more confusingly, a share price might perk up after revealing poor profits or a loss. The thinking may be that the bad news is now out of the way, things are going to get better and now is the time to buy.

In Chapter Six we will be looking at how you analyse individual shares. But first it is important to understand what influences the broad trend of the stockmarket. You don't have to be an economist – you'll find it's largely common-sense.

Read the newspapers, particularly the financial press, regularly and you will get a good idea of what people feel about the economy, where it is going, what the underlying economic trends are. All this influences the mood of the stockmarket.

When investors feel gloomy about the future, share prices tend to fall – this is what is known as a bear market. When they feel prospects are good or improving, share prices tend to rise – this is a bull market. These phases can last for several years although individual shares can 'buck the trend'. And while it is certainly true that the stockmarket tends to amplify and exaggerate underlying trends, these movements are based on what investors believe is happening.

Interest rates

Interest rates are crucial as we have seen all too clearly during periods when the high cost of finance has resulted in huge numbers of company and personal bankruptcies and falling profits and dividends. High interest rates slow down the economy, discourage consumers from spending and hit profits.

Low interest rates stimulate the economy as companies are encouraged to invest and expand and consumers take advantage of cheaper credit – all of which helps corporate profits. Although the impact of lower interest rates will take some time to work through, share prices will start to anticipate the upturn in corporate profits well in advance. Similarly, the stockmarket will get nervous when it sees interest rates rise.

One of the historical problems, however, has been that politicians have relied heavily on interest rates to alternatively ginger up or slowdown the UK economy.

Over the next few years we will all have the chance to judge for ourselves whether the decision to give control of interest rates to the Bank of England will prevent the 'boom and bust' cycle we have experienced in the past. At the end of the day it is steady long-term growth in the economy that is good for investors, companies and employees alike.

When it comes to picking individual shares, it's clear that some companies will benefit more, and sooner, than others from falling interest rates. If consumer spending looks as if it should pick up, the High Street retailers will be among the first to benefit, as will companies with large borrowings (so long as they are basically sound) – or industries like house-building that are particularly sensitive to interest rates.

The trend in interest rates is also important when it comes to deciding what kind of investments you should hold. When interest rates are high, fixed-interest investments like gilt-edged securities can look more attractive then shares.

At a time when business and profits are going to be under pressure, a high fixed return looks a safe bet compared to the dividends on shares which, as we have seen, reflect the trend in company profits. When interest rates show signs of falling, on the other hand, the prospect of rising dividends and capital growth, as the economy is stimulated, makes shares far more attractive to investors seeking the best returns.

Inflation

Shares can provide a good hedge against inflation. Providing the economy is reasonably healthy, company profits and share dividends can keep abreast of or better inflation, providing growth in the value of your investment as well as providing income in the form of dividends. While you can earn interest on a bank or building society account, the value of the capital may slowly be eroded by the impact of inflation.

Inflation is bad for the economy – and ultimately stockmarkets. Since the late 1970s and early 1980s, when inflation reached 20 per cent at one point, governments have become very conscious of the need to keep it under control. The main way they have done this is to put up interest rates and, as we have seen in recent years, that can bring the economy juddering to a halt with catastrophic results.

Exchange rates, too, are an important part of the investment scenario. Many major companies earn a substantial part of their profits abroad, providing investors with a spread of risk amongst a number of different economies. However, such companies are also susceptible to fluctuations in foreign exchange rates. Exchange rates also influence domestic economic policy.

For instance, our first ill-fated attempt to join the Exchange Rate Mechanism (ERM), designed to keep the EC currencies in line with each other – resulted in a long period of high interest rates as we struggled to keep the pound within the ERM. That was disastrous for UK business.

A fall in the value of sterling against other international currencies, such as we experienced when we came out of the ERM in autumn 1992, is a mixed blessing. It makes British goods cheaper abroad, providing an initial boost to exports. On the other hand it puts up the price of imported goods and raw materials, so it can be inflationary as well.

When the value of sterling rises strongly in comparison with other currencies, that is a problem for UK exporters, since it makes their goods look expensive to consumers.

There are, of course, a host of other economic indicators which influence the stockmarket – and no two commentators will agree on the various implications.

Other influences

Stockmarkets are sensitive to political and international events – the short term moves up and down can be alarming.

The UK stockmarket is influenced by what happens to other stockmarkets, too. Witness the events of Black Monday in October 1987, when a huge fall on Wall Street on the previous Friday triggered off a similar collapse of share prices in London and other international stockmarkets.

But what investors should look at is the underlying trend. There is a mass of information published every day. What's happening in the shops – are people buying? The retail sales statistics are published each month. What is business confidence like? The Confederation of British Industry (CBI) publishes regular surveys telling us what UK companies are thinking. Of course, these indicators lag behind events and you need to look ahead.

But consider the simplest share investment rule of all. **Buy when things appear gloomy**. Think about selling or switching investments when everyone thinks the boom is going to last forever. Its easier said than done, of course, and few investors are brave enough to buy right at the bottom and sell right at the top. But it illustrates how to use the information you have to anticipate what is going to happen longer term. And no one gets it right all of the time.

Trading systems

Two trading systems are currently operated by the London Stock Exchange. Traditionally, London has used a 'quote driven' system, where the prices at which investors wishing to buy and sell particular shares are quoted on SEAQ, the Stock Exchange Automated Quotations System. The broker then buys the shares from a 'middleman' known as a 'market maker'. This system continues to be used for most shares outside the FTSE 100. You can ask your broker to buy or sell shares 'at best' in which case he will buy or sell at the best price he can at the moment of the deal which, given minute by minute price changes, may differ a little from his original quote. Alternatively, when you place your order you can set a limit on the price at which you want to buy or sell the shares. The stockbroker doesn't have to buy that day – he may allow you to leave the order for him to execute over the next few days if and when the price matches the limits you have given him, although not all brokers offer this service.

In 1997 a new 'order driven' system changed the way in which shares in the largest 100 companies listed on the Stock Exchange (FTSE 100) and a few others are bought and sold, and it is anticipated that more will be traded through the new system in the future. Under the new system, you can place orders to buy and sell through your stockbroker who will then input your order on to an electronic order book to be matched. 'At best' orders are matched immediately at the best price on offer. 'Limit orders', which specify the worst price at which you wish the sale or purchase to take place, are matched in full or part immediately, or sit on the order book and wait for a match and trade to result. For most investors there should not really be a noticeable difference between trading shares through either of the systems. One advantage is that limit orders are easier for brokers to transact using the new system.

Since your buying and selling will probably be conducted over the telephone, you should ask your stockbroker to repeat the instructions just to make sure he understands what you want.

Bid, offer and spread

When you look at the share prices in the daily press you will see one price quoted. For shares outside the FTSE 100 it is usually the middle market price (i.e. the price midway between the last buying and last selling price) at the close of business the previous working day. For shares transacted through SETS (the official name of the new 'order driven' system) it is usually the price at which the last trade on the previous working day was transacted. It is not the price at which you can actually buy or sell the shares.

When you buy shares, you pay what is known as the offer price which is higher than the bid price that you will get if you sell them. The difference between the two prices is known as the spread. If you are buying shares in small or obscure companies, you should check the size of the spread. If it's wider than average it could mean the shares are not traded that frequently. When it comes to selling them you might find you get a poor price.

Share prices can change frequently during the course of the day depending on how many are being bought and sold through the market. When there are more sellers than buyers, the prices will go down. When there are more buyers, the market will move prices up. It's a question of supply and demand, the fundamental rule of any market.

SIX

LOOKING AT INDIVIDUAL SHARES

There is a mass of information available on individual companies whose shares are quoted on the stockmarket. A rundown of what is on offer can be found in ProShare's publication *The Investor's Guide to Information Sources*. The publication covers everything from daily newspapers to investment software to internet sites. Details of how to order this publication are contained in Chapter Seventeen.

Stockbrokers produce regular reports, the financial pages of newspapers comment on results, specialist publications like the *Investors Chronicle* carry in-depth analyses, share tips (to be treated with caution) and profiles of company chairmen. Stockbrokers who offer dealing services often have monthly bulletins for their customers. All of these make good reading for the interested and help enormously when it comes to picking and following shares.

The most comprehensive daily coverage of stockmarket and company matters is found in the *Financial Times* newspaper, which also gives the fullest list of share prices and daily financial reports and information. Many investors just buy the Saturday edition of the *Financial Times* as it provides a comprehensive summary of the week's events on the stockmarket plus personal investment advice. It also lists directors' dealings in the shares of their own companies, which many investors feel is a useful guide to prospects.

Aside from the *Financial Times*, there is daily financial and business news coverage in all newspapers, though some have larger sections than others.

If you invest in AIM or smaller company shares, you might not find much information on a regular basis. Most newspapers carry ever larger personal finance sections – usually on a Saturday and Sunday – but the coverage of individual shares, as opposed to unit and investment trusts, for instance, tends to be patchy. This is not surprising because the major fund management and insurance companies are very big advertisers in these sections.

But some newspapers do feature share tipping columns or personal stockmarket diaries on a regular basis. How investors should respond to them is a controversial matter. Obviously, the track record is a crucial point. What has happened to past suggestions? It's all very well if a share goes up immediately after it has been tipped in the press. But has it sustained and increased its price after that? It may well be a mistake to buy a share on a Monday that has been tipped at the weekend because the there will be lots of demand for the share and the price might be temporarily inflated. You may get a better price a few days later. Share tipping columns are worth reading because they provide a point of view – which you can agree or disagree with – and plenty of ideas. They are a useful way for a novice stockmarket investor to familiarise him or herself with the stockmarket, even if you don't follow the suggestions.

The *Investors Chronicle* is a long-established weekly magazine aimed primarily at the private investor, though it is also read eagerly by City professionals. It is a comprehensive guide to financial and economic events and issues. Most useful for investors is its coverage of company news and results and the statistical information and comment it provides on individual companies. There are also a number of monthly magazines available on the subject of investment including *Bloomberg Money*, *Moneywise* and *What Investment*.

There are also plenty of investment newsletters around, sold on subscription. Many of them specialise in small company, high technology or AIM shares and they can be very informative and useful. But subscribing to one or more of these can represent a major investment in itself, though you often see special offers for, say, a three months trial, advertised in the newspapers.

Private investors don't have access to all the instant data available to City professionals. The electronic news and share price services available in City offices are simply too expensive for the individual. But things are changing and there are now a variety of computer software packages and internet services available that enable investors to access stockmarket data through their personal computers. You can access daily financial news highlights free of charge through Ceefax and Teletext which also have regularly updated share prices available.

Much more elaborate, and much more expensive, are the company information services aimed at the private investor. The most comprehensive is probably *Company REFS*, which is available on either a monthly or quarterly basis. Pioneered by stockmarket guru Jim Slater, the service covers virtually all stockmarket companies, including those traded on the AIM, although the wealth of financial and investment statistics means it is probably too sophisticated for the novice investor. But if you get hooked on stockmarket investment, it is a valuable tool. Some libraries stock *REFS*. Other useful reference publications include *The Estimate Directory* and the *Major UK Companies Handbook*.

Company annual reports and accounts

It is also important to look at the information provided by the company itself to its shareholders. These are often complex documents which must comply with certain legal requirements. Yet the information contained in a company's report and accounts can be crucial if you are thinking of investing in a particular company. Many company reports look like glossy magazines, so full of photographs that it gets confusing. Others may be quite austere.

ProShare's *Introduction to Annual Reports and Accounts* is a simple guide to the main features in a company's report and accounts, explaining what to look out for and how to interpret the information, including a guide to financial jargon. Details of this guide and how to order it are contained in Chapter Seventeen.

Whatever the presentation, there are key features, common to all, that you should consider.

Profit and loss account

This tells you how well (or badly) the company traded during the year – how much profit it made and how much dividend it is paying. This will be shown side by side with the results for the previous year so you can make a comparison. Most of the important information on profits will already have been included in the preliminary statement, which is normally made available a few weeks before the publication of the annual report and accounts. The preliminary statement is released to the London Stock Exchange and the press, but not normally posted to shareholders. It gives the results for the year, but the annual report will give you a much more detailed picture of what a company has been doing.

An example of a typical profit and loss account is shown on page 54. Turnover means the amount of goods or services a company has sold. The annual report should disclose some interesting additional information – the proportion of sales overseas, for instance, and which divisions of the business are more important or achieved a better performance than others. You should look at the half-year interim results as well when you assess sales performance. Maybe sales slowed in the second half, maybe they are increasing faster. Obviously, retailers do most of their business over Christmas and the New Year. The annual sales figure is not necessarily the whole picture.

Specimen Profit and Loss Account

For year ended 31 December 1997	Notes	Current year £000s	Previous year £000s
Turnover	1	150,000	100,000
less Costs of sales	2	(116,500)	(84,800)
equals **Operating profit**		**33,500**	**15,200**
plus Net interest	3	200	150
equals **Pre tax profit on ordinary activities**		**33,700**	**15,350**
less Extraordinary items	4	(2,000)	(1,000)
equals **Profit before taxation**		**31,700**	**14.350**
less Taxation	5	(10,650)	(5,160)
equals **Profit after taxation**		**21,050**	**9,190**
less Minority interests	6	(200)	(150)
equals **Profit attributable to ordinary shareholders**		**20,850**	**9,040**
less Dividends	7	(10,300)	(5,000)
equals **Profit retained in the business**		**10,550**	**4,040**
Earnings per share (p)		**6.1**	**3.0**

To assess the trading profit – how much a company is making from its actual business – you have to look at the operating profit. Cost of sales and other expenses tell you how much a company has spent on running the business. It is a rough but useful guide to efficiency. If costs are rising in relation to sales, that could be a warning – or an indication or an area that could improve with better management. This includes the major item of wage costs, though details will also be shown separately elsewhere in the accounts. It may also include depreciation, the amount set aside to cover the wear and tear on plant and machinery. In theory, depreciation builds up a fund to cover the cost of buying new machinery when it is needed. Often there are numbered 'notes' to the accounts which include more information on specific items and provide more detail.

The leading indicator of a company's performance

Pre-tax profit is a crucial figure – the one that is widely regarded as the leading indicator of a company's performance. But before that figure is struck, the profit and loss account will show net interest which is worth looking at carefully. If a company has a lot of cash and few borrowings, interest received should exceed interest payments resulting in a plus for net interest. For most companies, interest paid will be greater than interest earned, causing a charge against profits. For businesses with heavy borrowings, movements in interest rates are an important factor when it comes to assessing future profits. If interest costs are way up, it could mean the company has more borrowings and overdrafts – or that interest rates have been much higher than previously.

The results of many companies will include adjustments for exceptional or extraordinary items – unusual gains and losses made during the year which are not part of normal trading activities. These might include profits from selling a factory or some other asset, the losses on closing a business and making redundancy payments, or the gain from selling a subsidiary company. These items are shown separately in the profit and loss account so everyone can see them clearly, and understand what they mean to the year's results.

Deductions and dividends

Tax is the next major item. Profits after tax or profit for the financial year show you what the company made from its year's trading after all costs, charges and deductions. This is what the company earned. After deducting any preference dividends, this is the figure used to calculate the earnings per share needed to arrive at the price/earnings ratio – the important investment yardstick described in Chapter Three.

Minority interests may figure next. These represent the part the profits or losses from businesses which the main company does not own completely, and so belong to outside shareholders. If that business is making a profit, the minority interest will be a deduction from the main company's profit. If it is losing money, then the minority shareholder has to bear part of the loss, so the minority interest should appear as a plus in the main company's figures.

Normally, some of the post-tax profit will be distributed as dividends to ordinary shareholders. The rest, shown as profit retained in the business at the bottom of the profit and loss account, will be reinvested in the business and become part of the assets shown in the balance sheet, which is the next item in the annual report that investors should consider.

Balance sheet

The balance sheet is not an infallible guide to a company's financial health. It shows what a company owns and owes on the last day of its financial year. You can be sure that it tries to look its best! Nonetheless, it is important to understand what the items in the balance sheet mean – how they can highlight a company's strengths and weaknesses. A specimen balance sheet is shown overleaf.

The first item is fixed assets – what the company owns in the way of land, property, factories, machinery, etc. The figure for fixed assets is not intended to show what the company would receive for these items if they were sold off. So remember, the real value could be somewhat different, particularly if most of the assets are plant and machinery. It is worth looking at the valuation for properties. If they have not been revalued for years, they might be worth far more at present day values.

Specimen Balance Sheet

Balance Sheet as at
December 1997

	Notes	Current Year £000s	Previous Year £000s
Fixed assets			
Land and buildings	10	5,000	3,000
Plant and machinery	11	20,000	15,000
Total fixed assets		**25,000**	**18,000**
Current assets			
Cash at bank		2,000	2,000
Debtors	12	15,000	12,000
Stocks	13	12,500	10,000
Investments	14	5,000	4,000
		34,500	**28,000**
less			
Current liabilities			
amounts due within one year	15	(14,000)	(12,000)
equals			
Net current assets		**20,500**	**16,000**
Total net assets		**45,500**	**34,000**
Shareholders' funds			
Share capital	16	34,950	29,960
Retained profits	17	10,550	4,040
		45,500	**34,000**

Current assets include the company's stocks, cash, investments and money owed by debtors. The figure for stocks is very important – if that moves significantly out of line with sales, you might wonder why. A big increase might suggest sales are not on target, or that the company has miscalculated demand. Or it might mean teething problems with a new distribution system. It costs the company money to hold stock.

It is always comforting to find plenty of cash or near cash in the balance sheet. As with the profit and loss account, you can make a comparison with the previous year. Movements in cash balances are also analysed in the cashflow statement which will be described later.

Current liabilities include the company's short-term borrowings – those it has to pay back within a year – and money it owes to suppliers and other creditors. High short-term borrowings might be a worry, particularly if the company's current assets do not include much cash. Running out of cash to pay the bills is how companies go bust, never mind how sound the assets may look.

After deducting these, and other liabilities, like long-term bank loans from the assets, the balance sheet gives a figure for net assets – what would theoretically be left to distribute to shareholders if the company sold everything and paid its debts.

When stockmarket professionals talk about 'asset backing', they mean how much these assets are worth per share. But as we have seen, it is important to study the balance sheet to see how the assets are made up and what they might really be worth. Clearly, it is more interesting from the investment angle if much of the asset value lies in cash or near cash or very saleable land or property. It is not so exciting if it is all in ancient plant or machinery, which often may be worth less than it seems.

Watch out for gearing

Assets and liabilities make up one side of the balance sheet whilst shareholders' funds make up the other side. These comprise share capital, reserves and the undistributed profits of the business built up over the years. These are effectively the capital which finances the business. A key point to watch is the proportion of borrowings to shareholders' funds, known as 'gearing' by the professionals. Acceptable gearing levels vary from business to business, but anything over 50% should be viewed carefully. It could mean a chunk of profits will be gobbled up by interest charges, leaving little available to pay dividends to shareholders.

Examine cashflows

The annual accounts will also include a cash flow statement – this is an important part of share analysis. It shows you how cash has come into the business over the year, and what use has been made of it. Cash is generated mainly from trading profits, but there may be sales of assets as well, or new share issues. It will show how this cash was spent – on buying assets and paying tax and dividends. The point of this statement is to see if the company has a good cash flow (hopefully the amount of money coming in will match or exceed the amount going out). By looking at the changes in items like stocks and bank balances shown here, you can learn a lot about the way a business is being run, whether it has sufficient working capital.

Don't forget the notes

Much of the substance relating to the profit and loss account and the balance sheet will actually be in the notes to the accounts. It is important to read these carefully. Before you do, take a few minutes to wade through the statement of accounting policies. It may appear hard going. But as you become more accustomed to accounts, you will begin to see that this can sometimes be crucial. It effectively defines what the figures really mean. Pay extra attention to any change in accounting policies from the previous year. There will be a good reason for it – and do not necessarily assume that, if some phrase is missing one year it has been left out by chance.

In their report the auditors state whether, in their opinion, the annual accounts comply with the law and give shareholders a true and fair view of the state of the company. Sometimes, however, auditors' reports are qualified – usually because the auditors do not agree with some of the accounting methods used. It is especially worrying when the auditors make reference to matters affecting the ability of the company to continue as a going concern. That means that the company has financial difficulties and could go bust unless its bankers, or other lenders, continue to support it.

The company will be well into its next financial year by the time the annual report and accounts is published, so the chairman's statement may contain some information on current trading – and more may be revealed at the annual general meeting. Shareholders can go to that and ask questions, if they wish, although this might not be possible if you hold your shares in a nominee.

The report of the directors will give you information about any changes in company business or structure and will show the board members' own shareholdings in the company and the names of anyone else with more than 3%. It also tells you about any options the directors have been given to buy shares. That is a useful way of boosting their rewards from the company. A reasonable options policy can be good for both board and shareholders.

SEVEN

WHAT'S A SHARE WORTH?

Open the *Financial Times* at the prices pages and you will quickly see that there are hundreds of shares to choose from. Many other newspapers also contain such financial information. Look more closely and each day there are some clear winners and a few nasty losers. The key to successful investment is telling one from another. But before you can do that, you need to be able to understand what all those columns of figures on the prices pages are telling you.

Vital statistics

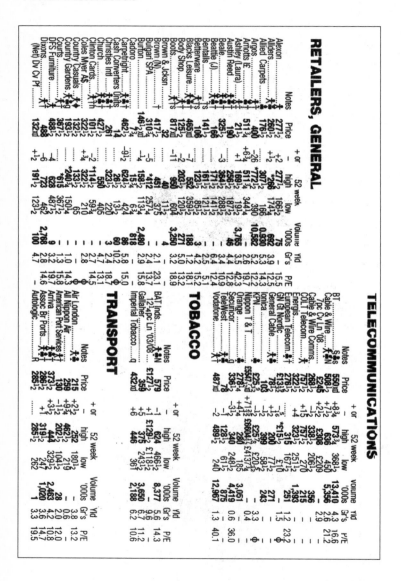

RETAILERS, GENERAL

	Notes	Price	+ or –	52 week high	52 week low	Volume '000s	Yld Gr's	P/E
Alexon	🯅	277½	+2	277½	166½	75	–	15.5
Allders	🯅♣	260½	+½	*266	174¼	692	3.9	12.5
Allied Carpets	♣	176½	......	307½	166	0.930	5.3	14.3
Argos	🯅†	400	–26	*772½	390	10,582	5.2	12.2
Arnotts I£	♣†	511¾	+6¾	511¾	344¼	–	2.6	19.7
Ashley (Laura)	🯅†	21½	+1	169½	19½	3,765	3.5	42.3
Austin Reed	🯅♣†	190	......	256½	187½	46	4.4	12.8
Beale	🯅♣†	325½	–3	364½	288½	–	3.4	10.9
Beattie (J)	🯅♣†	166	......	171½	141½	–	6.4	12.4
Bentalls	†s	141½	......	161½	121½	–	2.5	5.1
Betterware	🯅†s	106	......	123½	85½	3	4.2	15.2
Blacks Leisure	🯅♣†	465xd	–7	552	359½	188	1.2	18.1
Body Shop	🯅†	125½	–2	203½	120½	271	5.0	13.2
Boots	🯅†s	817xd	–11	950	604	3,250	3.2	18.9
Brown & Jcksn		32	......	40	11½	4	–	–
Brown (N)	†	417½	......	451	375	–	2.1	23.1
Bulgari SPA		310¾	–5	*412	257¼	–	2.4	13.7
Burton		146½xd	–¼	158½	113¼	2,480	2.9	15.8
Cadoro		7¾	......	15¾	6¾	818	–	–
Carpetright	🯅♣†	462½	–9½	624½	424	86	5.8	15.0
Cash Converters Units		14	......	26½	13½	60	10.2	Φ
Christies Intl	🯅♣†	261	......	323½	220	3	2.4	18.7
Church	🯅♣†	427½	......	550	405	–	4.7	13.1
Clinton Cards	🯅†h	101½	–2	*114½	59¾	–	2.7	14.5
Coles Myer A$		322½	+¾	322½	210	–	2.8	Φ
Country Casuals	🯅♦	132½	......	133½	65	–	–	Φ
Country Gardens	🯅♣g	193½	......	*240¾	150¼	–	1.0	14.3
Courts	🯅†	367½	......	*615	367½	–	1.3	15.8
DFS Furniture	🯅	488½	–4	628	487½	9	3.2	19.7
Dixons	🯅†	488	–6	723	462	2,768	2.8	14.6
(Net) Dv Cv Pf		132xd	+½	191½	123½	100	4.7	–

TELECOMMUNICATIONS

	Notes	Price	+ or –	52 week high	52 week low	Volume '000s	Yld Gr's	P/E
BT	§♣s	550xd	+8¾	573¾	368½	13,410	4.3	16.6
Cable & Wire	🯅♣N	508½	+7½	636	450	5,356	2.6	21.2
7pc Cv Ln '08		£245	+2½	£308	£209	–	2.9	–
Cable & Wire Comms.		268½	–½	338½	206½	356	–	–
COLT Telecom	🯅	757½	+15	757½	270	215	–	–
Energis		322½	+4	323½	251½	1,393	–	–
European Telecom.	♣†	276½	......	315	167½	251	1.2	23.2
GN Gt Nordic		£13 19/32	–5/16	*£15½	£10	–	1.5	Φ
General Cable	🯅♣	78½	+½	200	77½	271	–	–
Ionica		103	–½	399	58½	243	–	–
KPN	♣	£25 9/32	–½	£25⅞	£20 5/32	–	3.3	Φ
Nippon T & T		£5547 7/32xd	+71 25/32	£6604 17/32	£4137¾	–	0.4	–
Orange	♣	278¼	+4¼	280	185	3,051	–	–
Securicor	g	336½	–3½	340	248½	4,419	0.6	36.0
TeleWest	🯅♣	78	–1	128½	61½	875	–	–
Vodafone	🯅†	487xd	–2	489½	240	12,967	1.3	40.1

TOBACCO

	Notes	Price	+ or –	52 week high	52 week low	Volume '000s	Yld Gr's	P/E
BAT Inds.	🯅♣N	579	–1	624	466½	8,377	5.6	14.3
12¼pc Ln '03/08		£127½	+1	£129½	£118½	–	9.6	–
Gallaher		359	+5	375	243½	3,650	6.7	11.2
Imperial Tobacco	q	432xd	+6	446	361	2,188	6.2	10.6

TRANSPORT

	Notes	Price	+ or –	52 week high	52 week low	Volume '000s	Yld Gr's	P/E
Air London	🯅♣	215	+2½	252	180½	–	3.8	13.2
All Nippon Air		259	+9¾	462½	219	–	0.6	–
American Port Services	🯅†	130	–1½	202½	104½	28	2.0	12.0
Arriva	🯅♣†	373½	+3½	444	329½	2,463	4.2	10.8
Assoc Br Ports	🯅♣†	286½	+1	319½	247	1,020	3.6	14.7
Autologic	R	285½	......	285½	262	1	3.3	19.5

Pick any share. Going right to left across the columns you will find the previous day's middle market price (explained in Chapter Four). Then there is a column that shows you how the price moved yesterday – by how much it was up or down.

Then it gives you the highs and lows for the year. You can see how much it has moved up and down over the last year.

Next you will find the market capitalisation which shows the value the stockmarket puts on the whole company – the current share price multiplied by the number of shares in issue.

Then you have the dividend yield. This shows the percentage return on the share before income tax is deducted. It is calculated by dividing the gross dividend by the current share price and multiplying the result by 100.

The final column shows the price/earnings ratio (usually referred to as the p/e ratio) the other important investment yardstick explained in Chapter Three.

Stockmarket sectors

All shares are grouped under a particular sector. If you look at the prices pages, you will see a long list – textiles, property, hotels and leisure, food manufacturing, etc. This is not to remind you that Marks and Spencer is a retailer. It helps you find the price you want more quickly. And grouping companies into sectors provides an important tool for comparing the share price performance of different companies. Next, turn to the stockmarket report page in the *Financial Times*. There you will find a table of the FTSE actuaries share indices.

FTSE actuaries share indices

The FTSE 100 Share Index is the most widely used barometer of stockmarket ups and downs. It reflects the combined performance of the shares of the 100 largest companies listed on the London Stock Exchange.

There are other indices as well. The FTSE 250 charts the combined performance of the next 250 largest stockmarket companies below the top 100, while the FT Actuaries All Share Index shows the daily performance of the top 800 companies. It is a broader measure of stockmarket movements. And it forms the basis for the whole series of indices which reflect the price movements of shares in different sectors.

Sector indices

Indices like the FTSE 100 show you what the stockmarket is doing overall. But within that, shares in the various industrial groups may follow a different pattern. That is reflected in the various sector indices, which show the average movement of shares in that sector plus the sector's average dividend yield and price/earnings ratio.

All these different indices help investors to decide whether an individual share is worth buying, if it's time to sell and how well their portfolio is doing against the stockmarket as a whole.

Relative performance

As you begin to follow the stockmarket more closely, you will find that the professionals talk a lot about the 'relative performance' of shares as well as the overall trend. You will hear phrases such as 'this share is undervalued' or 'that share is overvalued'. Different sectors and companies may be 'due for a re-rating'. The shrewd investor wants to buy shares that are likely to outperform the rest of the stockmarket – that is, do better relative to the rest. The various indices we have outlined above act as benchmarks by which to assess individual share performance. They can also help pin-point shares that may outperform the rest of the stockmarket.

Say you spot a share in the food retailing sector. You have looked at the accounts and decided that it is a good or growing business. But before you buy you want to find out a bit more about the likely performance of the shares.

Price/earnings ratio

Is the price/earnings (p/e) ratio high or low compared with the sector average? It's low. That is interesting, but it does not mean that the shares are undervalued. A lower than average p/e ratio can indicate a number of things.

It might mean profits are expected to be down this year. When you work out the p/e ratio on the basis of reduced earnings per share, you may find it's bang on the average.

Or it could mean that even if profits are growing, they may be doing so at a slower rate than other food retailers.

The company may be small and, therefore, considered more vulnerable – compare the market capitalisation with the higher-rated companies in the sector – bigger companies may command a higher p/e ratio.

That is not to say the shares are not worth buying – it merely demonstrates that the p/e ratio reflects what the stockmarket feels about the shares. It is not expecting particularly scintillating profits growth. But feelings can change, so can companies.

If the company is entering a period of above average profits growth, then there may indeed be a 're-rating' of the shares in the future. This is the sort of thing every investor hopes to stumble on.

Maybe the share you fancy has a high p/e ratio relative to the sector. This does not mean it is overvalued. It usually reflects the fact that the company has had consistently higher than average profits and earnings growth – so far. What you have to judge is whether this is going to continue. Shares get re-rated down as well as up – a high p/e ratio makes them very vulnerable if profits fall short of expectations.

The private investor has to bear in mind the massive amount of research that goes on in the City. Stockbrokers' analysts and institutional investors are well placed to keep an eye on what is happening to leading companies. It's unlikely that you will come across a seriously-undervalued Blue Chip share, for example, that no one else has spotted. These companies are monitored very closely by the analysts.

But the different sectors and the major companies within them do respond to shifts in the economic cycle. At the first sign of a recovery, you might find that retail shares and house building shares are among the first to start moving upwards as the stockmarket anticipates a rise in consumer spending. That may be followed by a rise in the share prices of companies which supply the stores and make building materials and so will benefit from increased demand.

There may be a fashion for certain industries, often new ones, which look as if they are going to grow very fast over the next few years. The sector indices are a useful tool that show you what the stockmarket feels about that particular industrial grouping. Combined with your own judgement about future economic trends, it helps you decide if it is likely to underperform or outperform the stockmarket.

In Chapter Three we suggested that you pick a few shares for a hypothetical portfolio, monitoring them to see how they perform. Now is a good time to assess progress. You can compare your portfolio as a whole with the FTSE 100 Index. Would your shares have done better, worse, or kept up with the stockmarket average over the last few months?

Then have a look at each individual share. Did it respond to general news on the economy in the way you expected or to any results it may have announced meanwhile?

Now you have much more knowledge about the way the stockmarket works and values shares. Apply that to your hypothetical portfolio. Why have some shares done better than others? Are your original assumptions proving correct? Think about it carefully.

FINANCIAL TIMES
HEAVY RAIN FORECAST
BROLLY U-LIKE SHARES SOAR

EIGHT

COLLECTIVE INVESTMENTS

Many investors get their first taste of the stockmarket through buying unit trusts. These funds, which you will see advertised and written about in the personal finance pages of the national press, are a good alternative if you don't feel confident enough to pick your own shares. They are also useful if you want a broader spread of investments to balance a small equity portfolio. But buying unit trusts is not a way of avoiding having to use your own investment judgement. With well over 1000 funds on the market – some of them highly specialised – picking the right one requires some serious homework.

What is a unit trust?

A unit trust is a fund that invests in shares. When you buy 'units', you are acquiring not the underlying shares, but a stake in the whole fund which may own dozens of holdings in different companies quoted on the stockmarket. A unit trust's investments are looked after by professional managers who decide which shares to buy and sell. Unit trusts are often described as 'open ended'. As investors buy units, the size of the fund increases as it has more money to invest. If they sell units, the underlying investments can be sold. In practice, in normal markets there is a two-way traffic in units. Your stockbroker or financial adviser should be happy to make recommendations and buy the units for you.

Unit trusts versus shares

Over the last 30 years, unit trusts have been very popular with investors, even at times when fewer private individuals were buying individual shares. One of their main advantages is that they offer the small investors a good spread of investments at a reasonable cost.

Say you have £1,000 to put into the stockmarket. Because you have to pay a minimum commission each time you deal through a stockbroker it will be expensive for you to buy more than a couple of different shares. Maybe you are nervous about putting all the money in one or two companies. You might buy a unit trust instead. That will give you a stake in the wider range of stockmarket companies and you won't have to pay several lots of commission.

Unit trusts have another important advantage – they offer you an easy way of investing abroad. Buying individual shares in overseas companies is a bit daunting, but there are strong arguments for having some part of your investments in overseas stockmarkets. You would find it difficult to get into the Far Eastern stockmarkets, for instance, in any other way.

The major disadvantage is that putting all your portfolio into unit trusts takes a lot of the fun out of choosing your own stockmarket investments. And because funds invest in many different companies, no unit trust is likely to equal the performance of one real stockmarket winner – or indeed a real stockmarket disaster!

Picking unit trusts

Because there are so many funds, this is almost as tricky as picking shares. A number of publications including *The Investor*, *What Investment* and *Money Management* carry articles, details of what is available and performance statistics. Funds are divided into a number of different sectors – there is a wide range and they offer very different kinds of investment possibilities.

Even if you just want to buy into the British stockmarket there is a baffling number – growth funds, income funds, smaller company funds. There are international funds with shares in many overseas stockmarkets and unit trusts that invest in just one region like North America for example, or Japan. There are the highly specialised funds investing in gold shares, or property, or recovery funds where the managers select shares that have had a bad time but which they believe will now do well. And if you are really confused, there are unit trusts that invest in other unit trusts within the same investment management group. These are known as funds of funds. How on earth do you start? As with buying shares, you have to decide what kind of investment or combination of investments you are looking for.

If you want long-term capital growth, look first at the UK general and UK growth unit trusts. These make a sensible basis for any unit trust portfolio. Pick a broadly-based fund that has performed well and steadily over the last few years.

These funds will rarely feature among the top industry performers. But if you want a solid investment, this is where you should start.

If income is important to you, there are plenty of UK equity income unit trusts that invest in shares with above average yields – and give you capital growth, too.

International unit trusts are the best way to get a stake in a wide range of overseas stockmarkets. It means that your portfolio is not entirely dependent on what happens at home. But you should be aware that exchange rates can also have a big impact on the value of your investments. This is particularly important if you invest in just one country or region.

Like shares, unit trusts should be considered as long-term investments, making up the core of your portfolio. More active investors who are prepared to take a greater risk with part of their money should look at the specialist unit trusts on offer.

You will find recovery funds in the UK growth sector. Managers of these will be looking for the state of 'bombed out' companies shares with recovery potential – particularly interesting when the economy is climbing out of recession.

UK smaller companies are another, more volatile sector. These often do well in the final stages of a stockmarket boom.

Other cyclical sectors that you can invest in through unit trusts include property and gold shares.

Tracker funds

Tracker funds have become increasingly popular in recent years. These funds reproduce the performance of various indices like the FTSE 100 by buying holdings in all of the companies in the index or, sometimes, a sample of them. Tracker funds have become popular because many fund managers which 'actively' manage funds fail to outperform the index. The advantage of tracker funds is that they have low, if any, initial charges, and annual fees of just half of one percent. Do remember that they are as likely to track indices down as they are up, so they will not be so successful in a falling or 'bear' market. For this reason, tracker funds can take an important place in your portfolio but should not be the only investment you hold if you want to build a balanced portfolio.

Single country or region funds are another possibility. Through these you can invest in emerging markets or in developed economies like Japan, North America and Europe.

Remember that the narrower the investment range, the more volatile the fund can be. With specialist funds, timing is all important. If you manage to buy at the bottom and sell at the top, you can make handsome profits. Get it wrong and you can make hefty losses. You must know about the sector, be prepared to take a bit of a gamble. And be ready to sell if you think it the right thing to do. Above all, don't commit more than a proportion of your portfolio, a quarter say, to this kind of fund.

Costs

The cost of investing in a unit trust is included in the initial price you pay for your 'units'. The difference between the offer price at which you buy and the bid price at which you sell is usually around 6%. This spread covers the manager's own dealing expenses, and commission. In addition, an annual charge of between 1% and $1^{1}/_{2}$% is paid to the fund manager. It is a mistake to assume that it is always cheaper to buy unit trusts rather than shares – much depends on the size and spread of your personal portfolio.

Open Ended Investment Companies

Open Ended Investment Companies (OEICs) are similar to unit trusts because the fund can increase or reduce the number of units depending on the demand from investors. OEICs are relatively new here but have long been popular in Europe. The main difference is that they are companies, not trusts and there is just one price at which investors both buy and sell the 'units'.

Investment trusts

There are a number of similarities between unit trusts and investments trusts.

- Both offer investors a way of spreading stockmarket risks through pooled or collective investment.

- Both manage a portfolio of shares.
- Both offer a convenient route to overseas stockmarkets.
- Both offer a good range of investment possibilities, from reliable general funds covering the whole of the stockmarket, to more specialist categories of investment.

But there are important differences. Investment trusts are companies that have shares which are quoted on the stockmarket. What determines the price of those shares is not the value of their underlying portfolio, as in the case of unit trusts, but the demand for them on the stockmarket. This complication explains why they have not, until recently, been so popular with small investors. The price of a unit trust 'unit' directly reflects the stockmarket value of its portfolio. An investment trust share, on the other hand, usually sells at a discount to the value of its portfolio. The size of this discount can vary. That introduces an element of uncertainty into the investment equation. When investment trust shares were out of fashion a few years ago, the discounts grew very large – a third or more. Nowadays, they are much smaller, reflecting their increasing popularity with investors.

Naturally, the shares of well managed trusts where the fund managers have increased the value of their portfolio by skilful investment are in demand. The shares will go up as the value of the portfolio rises. In addition, the discount will narrow, so there is a double gain. Obviously, the discount means there is an element of extra risk, too – discounts can widen as well as shrink. Investment trust shares do broadly follow the progress of their underlying share portfolios. And they have some advantages over unit trusts.

Investment trusts can borrow money to invest. This gives investors greater growth potential – and higher risks. They can also invest in unquoted companies although these can be riskier investments. Investment trusts can be attractive take-over targets when their assets are worth substantially more than the market value of their shares.

Split capital investment trusts are specialist investments offering different kinds of shares depending on whether the investor wants capital growth or income. In simple terms, all the income from the shares in the trust go to one class of shareholder while the capital growth goes to another. These kind of investment trusts have a definite winding up date when the underlying investments can be sold. These are sophisticated investments with varying share structures. Potential investors should take advice from a stockbroker or IFA before buying.

Investment trusts have lower management charges, as a rule, than unit trusts. The bid/offer spread (i.e. the difference between the buying and selling price) for a large trust may be less than 3%. Shares are bought through the stockmarket. On larger amounts, commission costs can be lower than buying a comparable unit trust.

Your stockbroker will certainly be able to give you advice on what to buy. Again, *Bloomberg Money*, *The Investor*, *Money Management* and *What Investment* publish performance tables and commentary. As with unit trusts, your choice boils down to defining your investment profile and what kind of funds, or mixture of funds, are suitable for you. The same general rules apply.

Regular savings schemes for unit and investment trusts

Many unit and investment trusts offer regular savings schemes, which is a useful way of building up capital if you don't have a lump sum to invest. Many of these schemes offer minimum monthly investments of as little as £25, making them simple and cost effective for first time investors. To make things easier, the shares from these savings schemes are held in a nominee and regular statements are sent to you. You can also invest in them through a Personal Equity Plan. It is possible to exchange building society windfall shares for holdings in a unit trust or investment trust.

The Association of Unit Trusts and Investment Funds (0181 207 1361) and the Association of Investment Trust Companies (0171 588 5347) have helpful leaflets for potential investors.

NINE

BEGINNER'S GUIDE TO GILTS

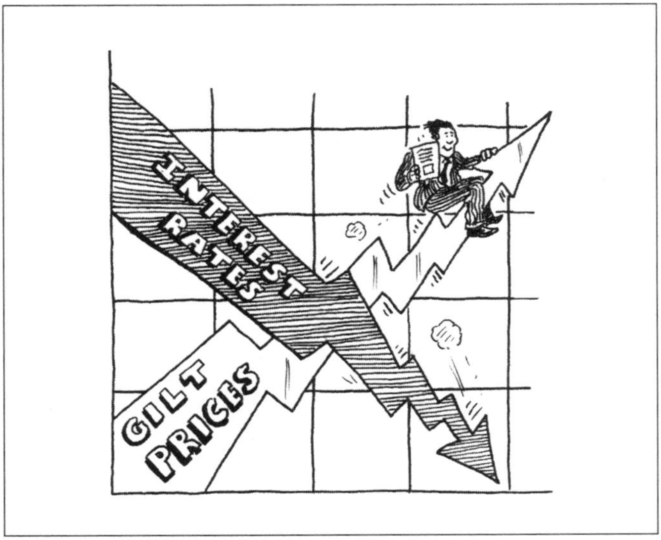

Shares are not the only kind of investment traded on the stockmarket. Government securities – or gilts as they're known – account for a large slice of daily market activity. But what are gilts? How do they differ from shares? What part can they play in your investment portfolio?

Gilts are a form of government borrowing. Selling gilts is one of the ways in which Government raises money to fund its spending programme. They are sometimes called Government Bonds.

Gilts are always traded in units of £100 nominal (or face) value. Gilts offer investors a fixed interest return – in the form of twice-yearly payments – and the promise of repayment of the nominal capital at a specified date. But it is important to understand that while government backing makes them secure investments with a certain and quantifiable return, gilts are not risk free. Once they have been issued, prices go up and down on the stockmarket. The key factors which make gilt prices move are the level of interest rates and the rate of inflation. Timing and anticipation are important when investing in gilts. In broad outline, gilt prices rise when interest rates fall, and fall when interest rates rise.

Investors can use gilts in two main ways:

- To secure a fixed return on their money over a number of years.

- To make a capital gain by buying gilts when prices are low, and selling when they rise.

Before we look at how gilts may fit into your own investment plans, it is important to understand the mechanics – and the jargon – of the gilts market.

Specimen gilts page from the *Financial Times*

Shorts" (Lives up to Five Years)

Notes	Yield Int	Yield Red	Price £	+ or –	52 week High	52 week Low
Treas Cnv 7pc 1997‡‡	6.99	6.35	100 3/32	......	101 9/32	100 3/32
Treas 8 3/4pc 1997‡‡	8.71	6.41	100 13/32	......	107 23/32	100 13/32
Exch 15pc 1997	14.57	6.43	102 15/16	–1/32	111 13/32	102 21/32
Exch 9 3/4pc 1998	9.58	6.54	101 13/16	......	105 5/32	100 1/32
Treas 7 1/4pc 1998‡‡	7.22	6.65	100 7/16	......	109 19/32	100 3/8
Treas 15 1/2pc '98‡‡	14.03	6.78	110 1/2	–1/16	118 17/32	110 1/2
Exch 12pc 1998	11.22	6.77	106 29/32	–1/16	111 13/16	106 29/32
Treas 9 1/2pc 1999‡‡	9.14	6.82	103 15/16	–1/32	106 21/32	97 11/16
Treas Fltg Rate 1999‡‡	–	–	100 7/32	......	100 5/16	99 7/8
Exch 12 1/4pc 1999	11.26	6.85	108 27/32	–1/32	113 9/16	108 25/32
Treas 10 1/2pc 1999	9.86	6.75	106 7/16	–1/32	110 11/16	106 11/32
Treas 6pc 1999 ‡‡	6.09	6.84	98 17/32	–1/32	99 1/4	96 19/32
Conv 10 1/4pc 1999	9.55	6.89	107 11/32	–1/16	118 19/32	106 9/32
Treas 8 1/2pc 2000	8.19	6.92	103 3/4	–1/16	104 5/32	103 1/32
Conv 9pc 2000‡‡	8.57	6.89	105 1/16	–1/16	107 1/2	103 29/32
Treas 13pc 2000	11.17	6.97	116 7/16	–3/32	120 15/16	116 3/32
Treas 14pc 1998–1	13.16	6.69	106 7/16	–1/32	113 3/8	106 7/16
Treas 8pc 2000‡‡	7.75	6.92	103 1/4	–3/32	104 29/32	102
Treas Fltg Rate 2001	–	–	100 5/16	......	100 7/16	99 3/4
Treas 10pc 2001	9.12	6.99	109 5/8	–3/32	112 25/32	98 29/32
Conv 9 1/2pc 2001	8.74	7.01	108 11/16	–1/8	109 9/32	107 7/16
Conv 9 3/4pc 2001	8.89	7.01	109 23/32	–1/8	110 11/32	108 1/2
Treas 7pc 2001 ‡‡	6.99	6.97	100 3/32	–1/8	101 1/8	97 15/32
Exch 12pc 1999–2	11.14	6.78	107 3/4	–1/16	109 5/32	107 23/32
Conv 10pc 2002	8.94	7.03	111 7/8	–7/32	112 5/8	109 31/32

Five to Fifteen Years

Notes	Yield Int	Yield Red	Price £	+ or –	52 week High	52 week Low
Treas 7pc 2002‡‡	6.98	6.93	100 1/4	–5/32	101 5/16	97 31/32
Conv 9 1/2pc 2002	8.62	7.04	110 3/16	–3/16	110 27/32	108 1/8
Treas 9 3/4pc 2002	8.74	7.04	111 19/32	–3/16	122 1/4	109 1/2
Exch 9pc 2002	8.29	7.07	108 19/32	–3/16	109 1/4	106 7/16
Conv 9 3/4pc 2003	8.65	7.06	112 3/4	–3/16	113 3/8	110 17/32
Treas 8pc 2003‡‡	7.64	7.00	104 25/32	–3/16	105 13/16	101 1/32
Treas 13 3/4pc 2000–3	11.59	6.97	118 21/32	–3/32	119 29/32	118 13/32
Treas 10pc 2003	8.73	7.07	114 1/2	–1/4	116 1/32	111 17/32
Treas 11 1/2pc 2001–4	10.05	7.03	114 15/32	–1/8	121 5/8	113 5/8
Treas 10pc 2004	8.64	7.08	115 3/4	–7/32	116 7/16	113
Funding 3 1/2pc 1999–4	4.04	5.83	86 11/16	–7/32	87 3/32	79 3/4
Conv 9 1/2pc 2004	8.35	7.05	113 27/32	–1/4	114 15/16	108 7/8
Treas 6 3/4pc 2004‡‡	6.85	7.00	98 1/2	–7/32	99 3/32	92 3/8
Conv 9 1/2pc 2005	8.30	7.06	114 13/32	–1/4	122 23/32	108 29/32
Exch 10 1/2pc 2005	8.67	7.08	121 1/16	–1/4	121 21/32	117 3/32
Treas 12 1/2pc 2003–5	9.80	7.07	127 9/16	–7/32	129 17/32	124 29/32
Treas 8 1/2pc 2005‡‡	7.80	7.06	109 1/32	–1/4	109 7/8	102 13/16
Conv 9 3/4pc 2006	8.27	7.12	117 7/8	–5/16	118 15/16	113 11/32
Treas 7 1/2pc 2006‡‡	7.29	7.07	102 29/32	–1/4	103 13/16	95 11/16
Treas 7 3/4pc 2006‡‡	7.43	7.09	104 11/32	–9/32	107 1/4	97 5/32
Treas 8pc 2002–6‡‡	7.72	7.14	103 11/16	–1/8	104 7/16	99 1/2
Treas 11 3/4pc 2003–7	9.69	7.07	121 1/4	–3/16	123 5/32	115 1/8
Treas 8 1/2pc 2007 ‡‡	7.73	7.10	109 29/32	–5/16	111 1/32	102 5/32
Treas 7 1/4pc 2007‡‡	7.15	7.06	101 3/8	–5/16	102 15/16	96 5/8
Treas 13 1/2pc 2004–8	10.09	7.11	133 27/32	–3/16	134 9/16	131 3/8
Treas 9pc 2008 ‡‡	7.86	7.11	114 15/32	–11/32	115 17/32	103 11/32
Treas 8pc 2009	7.48	7.14	106 15/16	–11/32	107 3/4	98 1/16
Treas 6 1/4pc 2010‡‡	6.78	7.16	92 5/32	–5/16	96 5/8	82 5/8
Conv 9pc Ln 2011 ‡‡	7.75	7.16	116 1/8	–3/8	117 3/8	105 11/16

Over Fifteen Years

Notes	Yield Int	Yield Red	Price £	+ or –	52 week High	52 week Low
Treas 9pc 2012‡‡	7.71	7.17	116 11/16	–13/32	118	105 1/2
Treas 5 1/2pc 2008–12‡‡	6.34	6.91	86 25/32	–3/8	87 15/32	76 5/8
Treas 8pc 2013‡‡	7.42	7.17	107 13/16	–13/32	109 1/8	96 1/2
Treas 7 3/4pc 2012–15‡‡	7.37	7.19	105 5/32	–3/8	106	94 3/8
Treas 8pc 2015‡‡	7.36	7.14	108 23/32	–7/16	109 15/16	96 13/32
Treas 8 3/4pc 2017‡‡	7.51	7.18	116 9/16	–15/32	117 7/8	103 5/32
Exch 12pc 2013–17	8.22	7.20	145 31/32	–3/8	146 11/32	138 3/8
Treas 8pc 2021‡‡	7.28	7.13	109 29/32	–1/2	111 7/32	96 3/32

Undated

Notes	Yield Int	Yield Red	Price £	+ or –	52 week High	52 week Low
Consols 4pc	7.41	–	54	–1/4	54 17/32	46 5/8
War Loan 3 1/2pc‡‡	7.19	–	48 21/32	–9/32	49 5/32	41 7/8
Conv 3 1/2pc '61 Aft.	5.34	–	65 17/32	–1/2	66 1/32	59 5/32
Treas 3pc '66 Aft.	7.58	–	39 9/16	–7/32	39 29/32	35
Consols 2 1/2pc	7.23	–	34 9/16	–7/32	35 1/32	30 1/16
Treas. 2 1/2pc	7.35	–	34	–3/16	34 9/32	29 13/32

Index-Linked

Notes (b)	Yield (1)	Yield (2)	Price £	+ or –	52 week High	52 week Low
4 5/8pc '98‡‡ (135.6)	–	2.82	114 1/32	......	114 3/8	113 1/16
2 1/2pc '99	1.97	3.15	181 11/16	–3/16	181 31/32	179 3/16
2 1/2pc '01 (78.3)	2.85	3.55	186 19/32	–5/32	187 11/16	179 9/32
2 1/2pc '03 (78.8)	3.08	3.59	182 7/16	–7/32	184 3/16	174 9/16
4 3/8pc '04‡‡ (135.6)	3.14	3.58	118 1/16	–7/32	120 5/32	114 11/32
2pc '06 (69.5)	3.27	3.60	192 11/32	–3/8	195 21/32	182 1/2
2 1/2pc '09 (78.8)	3.34	3.61	172 27/32	–13/32	176 9/16	163 13/16
2 1/2pc '11 (74.6)	3.38	3.62	179 1/16	–7/16	183 1/32	169 1/16
2 1/2pc '13 (89.2)	3.42	3.63	147 13/32	–3/8	150 31/32	138 15/16
2 1/2pc '16 (81.6)	3.44	3.64	157 15/32	–7/16	161 1/16	147 19/32
2 1/2pc '20 (83.0)	3.50	3.67	150 11/16	–7/16	154 9/32	141 1/4
2 1/2pc '24‡‡ (97.7)	3.52	3.66	124 31/32	–13/32	128 17/32	117 1/4
4 1/8pc '30‡‡ (135.1)	3.51	3.66	122 11/16	–3/8	126 3/8	115 21/32

Prospective real redemption rate on projected inflation of (1) 10% and (2) 5%. (b) Figures in parentheses show RPI base for indexing (ie 8 months prior to issue) and have been adjusted to reflect rebasing of RPI to 100 in February 1987. Conversion factor 3.945. RPI for October 1996: 153.8 and for May 1997: 156.9.

Other Fixed Interest

Notes	Yield Int	Yield Red	Price £	+ or –	52 week High	52 week Low
Asian Dev 10 1/4pc 2009	8.40	7.41	122	......	123 3/32	112 25/32
B'ham 11 1/2pc 2012	8.75	8.00	131 1/2	......	132 1/2	122
Leeds 13 1/2pc 2006	9.68	–	139 1/2	......	139 1/2	130 3/4
Liverpool 3 1/2pc Irred.	8.33	–	42xd	......	44	37 1/2
LCC 3pc '20 Aft.	7.89	–	38	......	39	32 5/8
Manchester 11 1/2pc 2007	9.02	7.65	127 1/2	......	127 1/2	119
Met. Wtr. 3pc 'B'	3.66	6.55	82	......	82	74 1/2
N'wide Anglia 3 7/8pc 2021	–	4.09	142 7/8xd	......	147 3/4	38 1/4
4 1/4pc IL 2024	–	4.47	138 1/16	......	142 15/16	32 3/4

● 'Tap' stock. ‡‡ Tax-free to non-residents on application. E Auction basis. xd Ex dividend. Closing mid-prices are shown in pounds per £100 nominal of stock. Prospective real Index-Linked redemption yields are calculated by HSBC Greenwell from Bank of England closing prices.

Gilt prices are shown in the daily financial section of many newspapers. In the *Financial Times* they are listed as British funds. The daily listings provide you with crucial information. As you will see from our illustration on page 83, each gilt has a coupon – the interest paid on each £100 nominal face value stock issued, and a redemption date – when that £100 will be paid back.

Confusingly, the coupon is not the real guide to the actual return investors get from a gilt. That depends on the price you pay for it. The price you will see in the daily list is what you pay for £100 nominal of gilt stock on the stockmarket. So to find out what your return would be at the current price, you must look further along the columns where you will see two kinds of yields.

The interest yield tells you what return you get if you buy the gilt at the current market price. This is also known as the flat yield.

The redemption yield tells you what rate of return you will get if you buy the gilt at the current market price and hold it until it is repaid. The redemption yield takes into account the capital gain or loss a holder of a gilt will make on repayment, as well as the interest paid. It shows you the total return.

Two examples

Looking at our illustration on page 83 you will see that Treasury 13 pc 2000 (Example A) priced at £116$^{7}/_{16}$ on the stockmarket. In other words you would have to pay £116.44 to purchase a holding of these gilts which have £100 face value.

All gilt prices are in pounds, not pence. The coupon is 13 per cent – that is the amount of interest you will receive on each £100 nominal of stock. But you are paying more than that nominal amount, so your actual return will be less – it will in fact work out at 11.17 per cent (i.e. 13 x 100 ÷ $116^7/_{16}$%). That is the interest yield or flat yield.

The stock for which you have paid £$116^7/_{16}$ will be repaid at its nominal value of £100 in the year 2000, so you will have a capital loss of just over £16 if you hold it until then. If you take that loss into account, your annual rate of return is reduced to 6.97 per cent if you hold the stock until repayment. That is the redemption yield.

Treasury 13 pc 2000 is what is known as a high-coupon gilt. The return is in the form of annual interest. As you look over the list we reproduce on page 83, you may wonder why anyone would want to buy a lower-coupon gilt, like Treasury 6 pc 1999 (Example B) for instance. But in the case of low-coupon gilts, the investment attraction is that what you may lose in interest, you make up as an assured return in the form of capital gain.

This gilt is priced at £98 – below nominal value. It will be repaid at £100 in 1999 at the latest. So while the interest yield is 6.09, the redemption yield is higher at 6.84, reflecting this capital gain. Since capital gains on gilts are tax exempt, low-coupon gilts are particularly attractive to higher-rate taxpayers.

The information provided by the daily financial press does the important sums for you. You have to understand what the figures mean and also the characteristics of the main categories of gilts you will see listed.

- SHORT-DATED gilts are those with less than five years to redemption.

- MEDIUM-DATED gilts are those with a redemption date of between five and 15 years.

- LONG-DATED gilts are those with over 15 years to redemption.

- UNDATED gilts have no set repayment date, and in practice are unlikely ever to be repaid. Take specialist advice before thinking of buying them.

- INDEX LINKED gilts were introduced in the early 1980s when inflation was a major headache. Both the interest paid and the capital repayment are linked to the Retail Price Index which provides investors with a degree of certainty and security if they hold to redemption.

Take the 2pc '06 index linked stock shown. 2pc is the coupon – the amount paid for every £100 of nominal stock. That interest payment increases every six months in line with the official rate of inflation. The value of the £100 nominal stock, due for repayment in 2006, is also adjusted in line with the RPI, giving it a current indexed value. The actual market price at which the stock is bought or sold will be at a discount or a premium to this indexed value. The actual redemption value, what the stock will be worth when it is paid back, is unknown, depending on the rate of inflation between now and then. So market prices for index linked gilts are governed by expectations of inflation.

These index linked gilts, it is fair to say, have been of more interest to pension funds than individual investors, but financial advisers sometimes recommend a holding to higher rate taxpayers as an inflation hedge for part of their capital.

The length of time to repayment is an important factor in gilt prices. 'Shorts', for instance, are more sensitive to the current level of interest rates.

Investors may compare the return on the short-dated gilt with the interest they might get from a building society or some other income-generating investment that matures within a few years.

'Longs' and 'mediums' are more difficult to judge since they require a degree of crystal ball gazing. While they offer the investor an assured fixed income for a number of years, you have to think carefully about the future level of both interest rates and inflation – particularly if you intend holding until redemption.

Usually you will find that the longer-dated gilts offer highest yields, reflecting the normal investment rule that the longer you 'tie up' your money, the higher the return. But you can get an 'inverse' yield curve where 'shorts' are showing higher yields. This indicates that interest rates are expected to fall – the lower yields on 'longs' reflect what the stockmarket thinks will happen in the future.

High inflation is not good news for conventional gilts, nor any fixed-income investment, because it eats into the real value of the income – and the real value of the capital at redemption.

High inflation inevitably means that gilt prices fall since yields must rise to compensate for the reduction in real returns.

Timing is also important when it comes to interest rates. If you go into gilts when interest rates are low, you stand to lose out when they rise because your return is 'fixed' when you buy – so you are missing out on a better deal – and the market price for gilts will go down as interest rates rise. When you consider the ups and downs in interest rates over the past few years, you will see why gilts can be a very volatile investment despite their 'safe' image.

The best time to buy gilts is when interest rates are high – and expected to fall. That way you secure a high fixed return (either in the form of income or capital) and have the option of taking a capital gain by selling your stock when interest rates fall and the market price rises.

Most investors who buy gilts are less interested in 'playing the market' by buying and selling gilts than in having a proportion of their portfolio with a guaranteed return on a medium to long term basis.

Choosing gilts

Which gilts you buy depends on your investment objectives – and your tax situation. Investors wanting high income should look for a high coupon gilt with a good interest yield and a redemption date that reflects the length of time you plan to invest for. If you retire at 60, for instance, and need a good income from your investments over the next 15 to 20 years, you will find an appropriately dated gilt among the 'longs' listed. There will be a capital loss if you hold to redemption. But that may be acceptable if your priority is maximising the ongoing income from your investments.

There may be less point in the high-income seeker buying short-dated gilts – even if the yield happens to be higher. But there can be no absolute rule. This is a complex subject, crucially influenced by timing, and many investors prefer to take expert advice.

For investors paying higher rate tax who do not need an immediate high income, low-coupon gilts are more attractive since most of the return will be in the form of a capital gain when the nominal amount is paid back rather than the annual interest. Capital gains on gilts are tax exempt and low coupon gilts can be a useful part of a growth portfolio.

While undated gilts are best left to the experts, carefully chosen index-linked gilts guarantee investors a 'real' return over and above the rate of inflation. Both the capital repayment and interest payments are linked to the movement of the Retail Price Index, so they offer the certainty of beating inflation. It is fair to say that index-linked gilts have not proved that popular in recent years when inflation has been seen to be under control.

Buying gilts

You can buy gilts through a stockbroker, financial adviser or a bank. As in the case of shares, there will be a minimum charge which will vary according to where you buy them. You can also buy the full range of gilts through the Post Office – ask for details of the National Savings Stock Register. Buying through the NSSR is not as cheap as it used to be, but with a minimum commission of £12.50 on purchases of up to £5,000 investors will probably find it cheaper to buy there than through a stockbroker. There is, however, no advice on offer.

Another advantage is that the interest on gilts bought through the NSSR is paid gross, that is, without deduction of tax.

Non taxpayers should certainly buy their gilts this way, though if you are a taxpayer you will have to declare the interest and pay tax on it eventually. If you buy your gilts through the stockmarket, tax is deducted from your interest cheque before you receive it and you must claim it back. From April 1998, however, investors will be able to receive their interest gross before deduction of tax.

TEN

TAX FREE INVESTMENTS

Over the past few years governments have been keen to stimulate personal savings. The result has been the introduction of tax concessions for certain kinds of investments. The principle behind this is that savers can invest up to a maximum sum and pay no tax on the proceeds.

Personal Equity Plans (PEPs) and Tax Exempt Special Savings Accounts (TESSAs) have proved hugely popular with the investing public since their introduction. In his first New Labour budget, however, Chancellor Gordon Brown promised a new financial vehicle designed to extend the principle of tax concessions for long term savings and investment.

Individual Savings Accounts (ISAs), as they will be known, are due to be introduced by April 1999, replacing PEPs and TESSAs. At the time of writing, a consultative document setting out the government's proposals for ISAs has been produced and this has caused much debate. Until the process of consultation is complete and the Government has agreed all the details of the new scheme, it is difficult to predict the precise effect it is likely to have on your existing investments or those which you might make between now and April 1999.

Bear in mind that the following details about PEPs and TESSAs are based on the schemes at the beginning of 1998. As the deadline for the introduction of ISAs gets closer, you should check carefully with your product provider or financial adviser to make sure you understand the likely benefits of investing in them further. You can also write to ProShare for a summary of progress on the development of the new ISAs.

Remember, it is also important to understand that you shouldn't invest just because of a tax concession. Choosing the underlying investment is still the most crucial decision. Unless that is sound, you are wasting your time and money.

Personal Equity Plans enable you to invest in the stockmarket and pay no income tax on your share dividends or Capital Gains Tax on your profits.

PEPs are offered by stockbrokers, financial advisers, unit and investment trust management groups, banks and building societies who are the plan managers.

How much can you invest?

Each individual investor can put up to £6,000 in any tax year in a general PEP, investing in shares or unit trust or investment trusts or a mixture of all three. And you can put a further £3,000 a year in a single company PEP – you put the money in the shares of just one company. So you can put a total of £9,000 a year into a PEP. If you don't use your maximum PEP 'allowance' each year, you can't carry it over to the next year, but bear in mind the 1999 ISA deadline. Once again the message is if in doubt, first check with your provider or product financial adviser.

You can't put an existing portfolio of shares or unit trust and investment trust holdings into a PEP – it has to be a new investment. But you have 42 days to put new issues or windfall building society shares into a PEP. As well as investing in shares, investment trusts and unit trusts, PEP money can be invested in corporate bonds.

Choosing a PEP

There are hundreds of PEPs to choose from. If you want a good spread of investments, a general PEP is your best choice and there is a wide variety. The basic choice is between a managed PEP, where the investment decisions are made for you, and a self select PEP, where you decide what shares or funds your money should be invested in.

- Are you looking for income? Some PEPs pay income quarterly or monthly. Corporate bond PEPs are intended to provide a high income.

- Are you looking for growth? Like unit and investment trusts, different plans have different investment objectives.

- Do you want just individual shares in your PEP?

- Do you want to put the lot into unit or investment trusts – or a mixture of these and shares?

- Do you want to make monthly contributions into a PEP instead of a lump sum investment? Some managers offer this facility.

With a 'managed' PEP, you should look for one with a good track record. Investment performance is more important than the level of charges in the long term. But remember that past performance is not necessarily a guide to future returns.

With a 'self select' PEP, you want one that allows you to switch investments cheaply and easily. These are offered by many stockbrokers.

You should look for a PEP that complements your existing investments. If you already have unit trusts, for instance, you might use your PEP to invest in individual shares. If you have a portfolio of shares, you might want to PEP a unit or investment trust instead.

TESSAs

A TESSA (tax-exempt special savings account) is a bank or building society deposit account. You can save up to £9,000 tax free in a TESSA, provided you keep the cash there for five years. You can invest up to £3,000 in the first year and up to £1,800 in the three following years and £600 in the final year. You will pay no tax on the interest. You can't withdraw capital without sacrificing the tax concessions, but you can get the interest, net of tax (the tax is repaid to you after the full five years).

- Look for the highest rate available. But remember that the rate goes up or down – there are very few fixed-rate schemes.

- Watch out for high 'penalty' charges on some accounts if you switch your TESSA to another bank or building society to get a better rate.

- You don't have to make a lump sum investment. Many banks and building societies offer monthly savings into a TESSA.

If you are thinking of opening a new TESSA don't forget to check beforehand with your product provider or financial adviser what the likely effect of ISA's introduction in 1999 will be.

National Savings

National Savings has a variety of investment products, some of which offer tax-free returns. You can get details and application forms from your Post Office.

Fixed Interest Savings Certificates

You can invest a lump sum of between £100 and £10,000 in each issue of Savings Certificates for a guaranteed tax free return after five years. Your capital is secure and you can cash in your certificates at any time, but you should hold them for the full five years to get the maximum return as the interest rate increases each year to maturity. When you compare returns on National Savings Certificates with what is available from banks and building societies, remember that the latter usually quote a gross return upon which you will have to pay tax. A higher rate taxpayer, for instance, would need a return of 10 per cent gross on a deposit to equal a tax free return of 6 per cent.

Index Linked Savings Certificates

Similar to the above, but the return is based on the rise in the Retail Price Index over the five years to maturity plus an increasing amount of extra interest each year. These should be of interest if you think inflation is going to start rising and a simpler, cheaper alternative to investing in Index Linked Gilts.

Insurance linked savings schemes

These schemes produce tax free returns for savers prepared to tuck their money away on a regular basis over the long term. The best known schemes are the with-profits endowment policies taken out to fund mortgages. But many other savers, attracted by a tax free return if the plan runs for the statutory ten years, find them a good way to build up a lump sum.

Money is invested in the insurance company's own internal fund and annual bonuses are added to your savings depending on how smart the fund management has been.

Before choosing a policy look up both the past investment record of the managers and the level of charges, which can eat up a lot of the investment value in the early years.

ELEVEN

PERSONAL PENSIONS

It cannot be said too often. A pension is one of the most important aspects of financial planning. Like your mortgage, your insurances and your 'rainy day' cash, making sure that you will have enough money in retirement must be a top priority – it is a cornerstone of your overall savings strategy. Even if you are already contributing to an employer's pension scheme – and happy to stay there – you should look carefully to see if you should make extra pension provision. If you are not, you should think seriously about investing in a personal pension plan.

Both this Government and its predecessor have been keen to promote the savings habit. When it comes to personal pensions, the tax incentives are very generous indeed, giving us plenty of incentive to save now for later. Not surprisingly, this has spawned a huge pensions industry – there are plenty of salesmen around enticing you to buy this or that plan. It can all be very confusing. Independent advice is often hard to come by. But here are a few general pension points to ponder.

Start early if you want to make sure of building up a decent pension to retire on. Each year you delay means that it will cost you more to create the same amount of pension at the end of the day. The sooner you invest the money, the more opportunity you have for your pension savings to grow over the years.

Inflation may be low now, but it is still a vital factor in assessing the real value of your future pension. Basic living costs will rise by the time you come to retire. What will that do to the spending power of what you are expecting to receive when you stop earning?

Your dependents will need to be looked after financially whether you die before or after retirement. Whatever pension scheme you choose, you must look carefully at these arrangements as well.

Everyone is now entitled to have a personal pension plan, even if they work for an employer that offers a pension scheme. One of the most difficult decisions is whether to join a company scheme, or to opt for the personal pension plans sold by a large number of insurance companies, investment houses, banks and other financial institutions. It is important to understand the basic differences between the two.

Company pension schemes

Company pensions may offer a pension based on the amount of your salary when you retire. These are known as 'final salary' pension schemes. Both you and the employer will contribute a percentage of your earnings to the fund. There will be a range of other benefits, too – a widow's or widower's pension, for example, and a life assurance payment to dependents if you die before retirement. There will also be the prospect of increases in the value of your pension once it is being paid. These are the plus points.

The main disadvantage is when you change jobs – the structure of company pension schemes favours those who remain in the same employment for a long time. Even though you can now take the 'transfer value' of your pension to a new employer, you may still lose out. Frequent job changes mean that you can end up with bits of pension from a number of past employers. An increasing number of companies are now switching from final salary to what are known as money purchase schemes. The amount of your pension is not linked to salary, but to the return on the 'pension pot' you have built up.

On the other hand, a company pension scheme, particularly a final salary scheme, is usually very good value for older employees who don't expect to move jobs before retirement. No one should opt out of an employer's scheme without taking independent advice. Most people are better off staying put. One of the tragic results of the liberalisation of pension regulations has been the number of people tempted out of final salary company pension schemes only to discover that the personal pensions they have bought may not match up in terms of the eventual benefits.

Personal pensions are best for the young who expect to change jobs several times during their working lives. And they are essential if there is no employer's scheme on offer with your job, or if you are self-employed. But it is essential to understand the difference between a personal pension and an employer's scheme. A personal pension means that you have your own individual 'pot' of money that you can contribute to as and how you like, regardless of who you are working for. The main disadvantage is that the employer does not contribute to the pension (though there is nothing to stop them doing so if you can negotiate it). And there is no guaranteed level of pension. What you get depends on the amount of pension, in the form of an annuity, that your 'pension pot' can buy you when you retire, rather than on the amount of your salary. It is a very important distinction.

Choosing a personal pension

There is a baffling range of personal pension plans on the market. And since the size of your pension depends on the amount of money you can build up, it is important to choose carefully. The first thing to consider is how you want your pension money, or premiums, invested.

Unit-linked pension plans give you a choice of different kinds of funds managed by the insurance or investment company. Typically, there will be a wide range of equity funds where money is invested on the stockmarket. These will include overseas shares – there will probably be a Far East or North American fund into which you can put your money. There is also likely to be a property fund, a fixed-interest and cash fund – and a managed fund which invests across the whole range – useful if you can't decide which to choose. You may also be offered a 'tracker' or index fund which aims to match a specific stockmarket index – the FTSE 100 for instance.

Clearly, you want to look hard at the investment performance of these funds, bearing in mind that short-term ups and downs may not mean very much when you are tucking away money for the long haul. The further it is until retirement, the more risk you may be prepared to take – investing in equity funds, for instance. But the nearer you get to retirement, the more predictability you need. Then is the time to secure your stockmarket gains by putting your money in the cash fund, for example. You can switch your money between different funds. If you go the unit-linked route, you will need all your investment knowledge to make the most of your money.

With-profits pensions plans invest the premiums in the insurance or investment company's own fund – which will be mixture of shares, gilts and, maybe, property. You will be guaranteed a minimum amount plus, each year, a share of the profits of the investment fund. The crucial difference between this and a unit-linked pension plan is that these profits, once given, cannot be taken away – and you should get a final bonus added to your fund when you retire. Again, it is important to look at the bonus record of the pension provider, though this is no cast iron guarantee of what will happen in the future.

The ideal way to invest your pension money is to use both types of plan – the unit-linked to give you the opportunity for capital appreciation in the stockmarket – and the with-profits to provide a more secure, predictable investment. It is always sensible to spread the risks when you invest and this principle applies equally to your pension plan.

There is nothing to stop you taking out more than one pension plan, though you should enquire about the level of charges, which can vary enormously. But bear in mind that in the long run investment performance will be more important. From the personal discipline point of view, a regular-premium policy where you make contributions each month or year is a good idea. But you can make a series of one-off payments through single-premium plans instead, or use them to top up your pension payments as and when you can afford it.

How much to invest?

Sellers of pension plans will present you with a battery of figures about how much pension your contributions will buy you in 20 or 30 years' time. It is important to understand that these are only estimates, based on assumptions about investment performance. They are not promises or guarantees. You also have to think about the impact of inflation on the rather attractive amounts of pension that are illustrated. The important point to remember is that the sooner you invest, the more chance your pension savings have to increase in value. Even if you can make only modest contributions initially, you can increase these later on as you earn more money and have fewer financial responsibilities.

Tax

One of the most attractive features of saving through a pension scheme is the generous tax concessions. You can get full tax relief on your pension contributions up to a maximum proportion of your earnings. And the older you are, the higher the proportion of your income you can pay in under present Inland Revenue rules. For instance, you can get full tax relief on up to 17½% of your taxable earnings if you are 35 or younger – but this proportion rises in stages the older you are. At age 51, for example, your limit will be 30%. So you should check what your limit is with the tax man.

If you are employed, you will make contributions to your personal pension plan net of basic-rate tax and claim any higher-rate tax relief from the tax man. If you are self-employed you will make your contributions gross and claim the tax back on your tax return form.

If you don't invest up to the maximum in the tax year – and few of us do – you can make it up later on when you have more money. You can go back six years and utilise any unused tax allowances as well as getting your maximum tax relief for the current year.

Additional voluntary contributions (AVCs)

If you are in an employer's scheme but you want to put more money into your pension, you can do so through an AVC. First you have to look at what percentage of your earnings you are already contributing. You can get full tax relief on extra contributions provided the total that you contribute is not more than 15% of your earnings. Many employers offer an AVC scheme of their own, but you are perfectly entitled to buy an independent one from any insurance or investment company of your choice. If you opt for an employer's AVC, there should be no charges – but you should enquire carefully about the terms – exactly what are your extra contributions buying you? If you buy a free-standing AVC from an insurance company, you will pay commission. It may be worth it if the benefits look better. Compare deals to find out what is appropriate.

The tax concessions on pension contributions – whether you are taking out a personal pension plan or 'topping up' with an AVC – make them a very attractive way of saving money. But while you should make sure you are building up a decent pension, it is a mistake to make this your only form of saving. Pensions are inflexible compared with other kinds of investments. Although you can take some of your money in a lump sum, the rest has to be paid as pension. What you get in the end depends on how long you, or your dependents, live.

It is not the same as having, for example, a portfolio of shares or unit trusts that you can cash in when you want. For this reason, many investors prefer to have a PEP, for instance, rather than an AVC. It is important to strike a balance.

TWELVE

TAX

Tax can be a complex subject. The application and impact of tax laws can vary widely from case to case. For this reason, this book can only provide general guidance and, if you are concerned about your tax position, you should consult a professional adviser such as a chartered accountant. The Inland Revenue also produces a range of easy-to-understand booklets which are available free of charge from your local tax office.

Never invest in something just because of a tax break. But this does not mean that you can completely ignore the tax factor when it comes to your investment strategy. As an investor, you can be taxed in two ways, on income from shares and tax payable on the growth in the value of your investments when you come to sell them. It is vital to know the basic rules, and how you can, quite legally, reduce your tax bill by organising investments in the most efficient way

If you have your own business, or a large investment portfolio, you may have access to professional tax advice – but all investors should have a working knowledge of the way taxation policies affect them. Particularly as the new Self Assessment system puts more responsibility on taxpayers, themselves. There are important differences in the tax treatment of the various investment products, too.

Tax free investments

'Tax free' investment means just that. You are not liable for tax on your investment returns. Examples include many of the National Savings products, TESSAs – the tax-exempt special savings accounts offered by banks and building societies – and PEPs, the personal equity plans offered by most financial institutions. Provided you stick to the rules, all returns – whether in the form of income or capital – are tax free to the investor. The new Individual Savings Account, which the Government intends to introduce in 1999, will rationalise and extend the principle that people can be encouraged to save by offering them tax free returns. Tax free investments, however, don't offer any tax concessions on the money you put into savings. At the moment, you can only get tax relief on money you put into a pension plan.

Some investments pay income gross to investors, without the deduction of tax. Examples include the National Savings Investment Account, gilt-edged securities bought through the National Savings Stock Register at the Post Office (and on all holdings of gilts from April 1998) and income from offshore deposits. But this does not mean that you are not liable for tax on this investment income. You are, unless your total income is so low that you don't pay tax at all. This subject has been dealt with in some detail in Chapter Ten.

Tax on income from investment

Most investment income is paid net to investors, after deduction of basic-rate tax. Examples include dividend payments from shares and interest on bank and building society accounts. Basic-rate taxpayers will have no more to pay on income from shares, unit trusts or bank and building society accounts – you will receive the income net of basic rate tax. In the case of income from shares, the dividend payment voucher, which you must be careful to keep, will state the amount of tax deducted. Under the present rules this is 20%, the present level of lower-rate tax – even though the basic rate is 23% you will not owe any more. Remember, you will have to pay tax on any interest received gross – where no tax has been deducted.

The position is different if your total income means that you are in the higher tax band (currently 40%) where you will owe an additional amount to the tax man. Say your actual share dividend payment is £80 after the deduction of 20% tax. The gross amount is £100. If your top tax rate is 40%, your tax liability on it will be £40, 40% of £100. You have already had £20 deducted, so you will have to pay the tax man another £20. Income from bank or building society accounts will also be taxable at 40%. At present basic-rate tax of 23% is deducted before you receive it. So a higher-rate taxpayer will owe another 17% to the Inland Revenue.

The Government has announced a change in the situation regarding tax on dividends, which will come into effect in April 1999. Non-taxpayers (children, non-earning wives) can claim back the tax deducted from bank and building society interest and dividends, or ask for the payments to be made gross without deduction of tax.

Married couples may be able to reduce their total income-tax bills by organising their investments in a tax-efficient way. The current system of independent taxation means that both partners can claim personal tax allowances. If one partner, perhaps a wife looking after children, is not earning, it would make sense to transfer income-producing investments into her name. Provided that her income is not higher than the level of the personal allowance, she can claim back the basic-rate tax deducted from investment returns. If both partners are earning, but only one of them is a higher-rate taxpayer, the same principle applies – investments should be organised in such a way that income is paid to the basic-rate taxpayer – reducing the size of the overall tax bill.

Tax on growth in value of investments (CGT)

Capital Gains Tax (CGT) is payable on the increase in the capital value of your investments when you sell them. Shares are the obvious example. In the case of building society 'windfall' shares, the purchase price will be taken as nil. The rate of CGT you pay depends on your own top rate of income tax, but a generous annual exemption, currently £6,500, means that many individual investors should pay little or no CGT.

It is very important that you keep up-to-date records of all your investments – the prices at which you buy and sell shares and the income you receive from them. If you do that, it should not be too difficult to work out how much, if anything, you owe the tax man. Here are some important points to note when calculating CGT:

- You can make profits of up to £6,500 during the tax year without paying any CGT at all.

- You can offset any losses against your capital gains in the same tax year. For example, if you have sold shares at £8,000 profit, but have taken a loss of £3,000, your overall profit will be reduced to £5,000 – well below the level of the CGT exemption.

- You can offset capital losses against gains in future tax years.

- You can only use the CGT exemption for that current tax year. You can't carry it forward to use in future years.

Capital gains are index-linked for tax purposes. That means the paper profit is reduced by the amount of inflation recorded since the purchase. If you are well within your CGT exemption limits, index-linking the gain is rather academic. ProShare's *Investor Update* number 9 RPI 'Figures for CGT Calculations' is a useful source of information. ProShare also produces a *Portfolio Management System* which enables you to keep an accurate record of your share transactions and simplifies accounting to the Inland Revenue. See Chapter Seventeen for further details of how to obtain ProShare products and services.

How to make the best use of the ground rules

These ground rules provide scope for reducing your tax bill with some easy planning. It's important to note that married couples each have their own CGT exemption. Investments should be divided to take full advantage of this generous rule.

Your portfolio should be reviewed carefully towards the end of each tax year in order to use the annual CGT exemption. If you have built up large profits in one share, you might want to take them or offset them with some of your losses. It doesn't mean that you have to abandon what you still believe to be a good investment. You can sell them to establish a profit in the current tax year that will use your CGT exemption and then repurchase them. Ask your stockbroker about 'bed and breakfasting' – the market term for this widely-used procedure.

THIRTEEN

NEW ISSUES, TAKE-OVER BIDS, RIGHTS AND SCRIP ISSUES

Many people became shareholders for the first time when they bought shares in British Telecom, British Gas and other major privatisations. Millions more became shareholders when their building societies turned themselves into banks and floated their shares on the stockmarket. The privatisations and the building society flotations were both New Issues, but bigger and more spectacular examples of how companies come to the stockmarket.

Going back to the basis of the stockmarket, selling shares in a company is the alternative to borrowing money from the bank to finance expansion. Offering your shares to the public encapsulates the original capital-raising function of the stockmarket. For investors it is an opportunity to buy shares without paying commission and to get them at an attractive price.

Unfortunately, many companies now make their stockmarket debut through what is known as a placing. Shares are sold to financial institutions and its difficult for individual shareholders to get a look in unless they approach the stockbroker who is helping to organise the float. The placing is a cheaper and more convenient way for companies to go to the stockmarket.

In an offer for sale, shares are offered through newspaper advertisements at a fixed price. You can apply for the prospectus which gives you details and the prospects for the company. ProShare's *Guide to Broker's New Issue Services* is a useful guide to the services offered by retail stockbrokers to individuals who wish to gain access to new issues. see Chapter Seventeen for details.

Assessing new issues

If you do spot an offer for sale you like, the safest way of assessing it is probably press comment. Newspapers do get it wrong sometimes, but they usually have a good idea whether the company is a goer or a flop. Lots of good publicity usually ensures a successful flotation, but not always. Companies and their advisers want to be sure that there will be plenty of takers for the shares, so they try and price them at a level that will show a profit on the first day of dealings. This profit is known as a premium.

Look carefully at the prospectus. Compare the price earnings ratio and dividend yield of the company with other companies in the same line of business. A new issue should be valued a little lower than its established rivals. It is worth looking at who is sponsoring the issue, which merchant bank or stockbroker. A reputable name counts for a lot, as do earlier new issue successes.

If a new issue is very popular, it may be oversubscribed. This means there are more applications for shares than there are shares on offer. In this case, the issuing house may simply hold a ballot – a lucky dip – to decide who gets shares, and everyone else is excluded. In the big privatisations issues, potential investors were 'scaled down' – they received less shares than they asked for. Of course, things can go wrong with a first time flotation even if the company looks solid enough. Unexpected bad economic news can depress the stockmarket in the vital days between the announcement of an offer and the time dealings actually start. In that case, the shares may fall below the offer price, going to what is known as a discount. Surplus shares are taken up by City institutions who have agreed to underwrite the new issue. It can take the shares a long time to recover from a disappointing debut on the stockmarket.

Take-over bid

When a company finds itself on the receiving end of a take-over bid, it can mean a nice bonus if you happen to be a shareholder.

To get you to accept their offer, the bidder will offer an amount in cash or shares, or a combination of the two, worth more than the current stockmarket price.

A contested bid may prove a bonanza as the bidding company may have to increase its offer in the face of fierce resistance from the board or a counter bid from another predator.

Take-over activity tends to go in cycles – witness the explosion in activity in the 1980s when huge take-overs hit the headlines. When the stockmarket is going strong, companies on the prowl can use the enhanced value of their shares to make acquisitions. When the share prices are weak, take-overs become less popular.

Identifying bid targets

Investors should keep an eye out for likely bid targets to add a bit of speculative spice to their share portfolio. Read the financial press – there are often bid rumours reported which may be worth investigating, and look for other signs.

These might include the acquisition of a large block of shares in a company by another group, which may herald the start of a take-over. Sometimes the stake is sold on. Sometimes the purchaser just sits there with it. But sometimes a bid does materialise, though you can never bank on it.

Companies held back by uninspired management may be a bid target. If a company seems to be lagging behind its sector rivals, find out why. Another company may well see an opportunity to make more money out of a basically sound business that is poorly managed. Companies that are weighed down by loss-making divisions, heavy borrowings or over expansion are vulnerable to take-over. A predator may see a good financial opportunity in reorganising the business by cutting losses and selling off the profitable parts.

When a take-over bid is announced, you do not have to do anything immediately. If it is opposed by the existing board, you will receive masses of propaganda from both sides over the next few weeks. And you can be pretty certain that the first offer made will be increased. Even if the bid is agreed by both sides, there is always the chance of a higher counter offer from another company. Keep an eye on the market price of the shares. If it is higher than the value of the offer, it tells you that a better one is expected. Even if no rival bidder emerges, the predator often has to improve on the initial offer to secure acceptance from the big financial institutions.

The only thing to worry about at this stage is the possibility of the bid being referred to the Monopolies and Mergers Commission which keeps an eye on take-overs and mergers. A reference usually kills the bid stone dead because it means months of investigation. If you think there is a strong chance of a referral, you might want to sell your shares in the stockmarket while the going is good.

There are all kinds of City rules and regulations on take-overs, most of which need not concern individual investors. The official offer document you receive will set out the terms of the bid and the closing date for acceptance.

There is little point in accepting at once, although if you accept and the bidder is later forced to make a higher offer, you will get the higher offer in most circumstances, so you do not lose out. But while there is the chance of a rival bid, there is nothing to be lost by waiting. At some point, however, you are going to have to make some decisions.

Decision time

Not all bids succeed. Some companies have mounted successful campaigns to keep their independence in the face of a take-over attempt, getting the backing of loyal shareholders. What you decide is up to you. You must look at the detail of the offer. It may be all cash or all shares or a combination of both. Often there is an offer of shares with a cash alternative. You have to choose.

The value of any share offer to you depends on the market price and prospects of the bidding company. Often its share price falls a little during the course of a bid. You have to consider whether you want shares in the company. The advantage of taking a share offer is that you are not liable for Capital Gains Tax when you swap. This is important if you have built up a sizeable profit on your holding.

If you take a cash offer, you might be liable for CGT. Much depends on the amount of profit you will make by accepting the cash and the way you use you annual CGT exemption. On the other hand, cash means certainty – you know exactly how much you are going to get. But before you accept a cash offer, you should compare it with the value of your shares on the stockmarket. If it is higher, sell there instead.

Rights issues

When a quoted company wants to raise money it can either borrow from the bank or ask its shareholders to put up the cash by buying more shares. The latter is obviously the cheapest option for the company. But a rights issue, as it is called, is rarely popular with shareholders who regard it as an occupational hazard of stockmarket investment.

But it is not necessarily all bad news. Rights issues can result in a substantial fall in company borrowings and interest, which benefits profits and earnings. Rights issues can be a good way of financing expansion. Alternatively, a rights issue may be a response to a crisis, launched as a last-ditch effort to save a company from going under. Whether you take up your rights to the shares or not may depend on what you feel about the company's prospects. You will be sent a document detailing the offer and telling you how the money will be used. You can find out what the market thinks about the rights issue by reading the press or asking your stockbroker.

You will be offered new shares in proportion to the amount you already have. So a rights issue may be one share for every three or four or five you hold. The price of the new shares will be below the current market price – 20% is a rough average – to entice you to buy. But the announcement of a rights issue will have an immediate effect on the value of your existing holding. The share price may fall initially – by how much depends on the size and the terms of the issue. The adjusted price is called the ex-rights price.

But there is no reason why individual shareholders should buy new shares if they do not want to. If the company is basically sound, the financial institutions will have them. But you have to face the fact that, at least for the moment, the value of your holding may well be less and the company's earnings will be diluted. Alternatively, you may welcome an opportunity to add more shares to your holding without having to pay dealing costs or stamp duty.

Here are some points to watch. Some rights issues flop because the big financial institutions do not want them. If the price of the new shares is very near or above the price quoted on the stockmarket, something is wrong and you normally should not buy them. If you do not want the new shares, you may be able to sell your 'nil paid rights' in the stockmarket for a handy profit. Ask your stockbroker – and find out first if it is worthwhile once you have paid his commission.

If you do nothing, the company will eventually sell your nil paid rights for you and send you a cheque, if there is a profit in it.

Scrip issues

Scrip, or capitalisation, issues are different from rights issues. You don't pay for the new shares, which is why they are sometimes known as bonus issues. But, as with rights issues, you get extra shares in proportion to the amount you already own – one for three – for example. The company merely increases its nominal capital and the market price of the shares adjusts to take account of the increased number of shares. Companies have scrip issues when they feel their share prices are getting too heavy.

Individual investors seem to like having scrip issues – they can sometimes perk up the market price a bit. But remember to mark the changed prices carefully in your records, for a forgotten scrip issue can seriously muddle your calculations.

FOURTEEN

YOUR SHARE PORTFOLIO

There are theories galore about picking shares. Every expert has a system. It might be based on looking at company data, analysing trends, or sticking a pin in the prices pages of the *Financial Times*. But running a successful share portfolio is not just about picking winners. It's about organising your investments to help you achieve your personal financial objectives.

- What kind of return do you want?
- How much risk can your nerves stand?
- Do you need income now?
- Or are you investing for a nest egg in the future?

Everyone has different requirements. But there are several broad categories that cover most stockmarket investors. And the way you handle your portfolio depends on how you see yourself.

- *You earn a comfortable income with a pension, but you want to build up some capital. You don't have a lot of time to devote to the stockmarket and you don't like taking big risks.*

You need a share portfolio to give you long-term capital appreciation and reasonable security. A mixture of Blue Chips and growth shares would be appropriate plus some unit and/or investment trusts.

Your share portfolio will not be particularly active. But you need to make sure that you are beating inflation and at least doing as well, if not better, than the stockmarket as a whole.

- *You are nearing or in retirement and you want to secure high-income return from your investments.*

You need to put a proportion of your capital in gilts and other fixed-interest investments when interest rates are high. Timing this well is very important. Your share portfolio should include higher-yielding shares and Blue Chip companies. Even if income is your chief objective, your equity portfolio will be the main way to protect your capital from inflation and to supplement your income by taking some profits when interest rates are low.

- *You really enjoy playing the stockmarket and are prepared to spend time studying it. Even if you want to get a significant income out of your portfolio, you may well choose to do it by investing for capital growth and taking profits on a regular basis.*

Your share portfolio should reflect your active interest. You might opt for a selection of growth stocks plus special riskier situations – penny shares, prospective bid candidates, recovery stocks, and so on. But be sure that you have the time and interest to keep a careful eye on them day to day. And only speculate with money you can afford to lose.

Whatever kind of investor you feel you are, there are some general rules of portfolio management that apply to all.

Spread the risks

Whatever your circumstances, you need to have enough different shares to give yourself a reasonable spread of investments. Even if you are going entirely for Blue Chips you must spread the risk as even the most solid companies can hit a bad patch. Aim to hold a handful of different shares. You should invest in several sectors rather than concentrating on just one. This doesn't mean that you shouldn't have more invested in, say, retailing if you think there is a recovery in consumer spending on the horizon. Just do not put all your eggs in one basket.

On the other hand, don't have too many shares. It will be a headache keeping track of them all. How many different shares you hold depends partly on the amount of money you have to invest. Dealing in very small quantities can be expensive because of minimum commission rates. Half a dozen to a dozen shares is a rough guideline for most private investors. Ideally, aim to invest at least £2,000 or certainly not less than £1,000 in each company in your portfolio. Invest less and commission charges will be proportionately high and your investments will have to work very hard to make a profit.

Check your portfolio

Get in the habit of checking the progress of your investments on a regular basis, noting movements in prices daily, weekly or monthly. It will give you some feel for the way certain shares or sectors react to general movements or events. It will show you which shares are earning their keep and which are lagging behind. And shares which move against the trend – fall when the market rises, or rise when it falls – are giving you a buy or sell sign well worth heeding. However, you should not pay too much attention to daily stockmarket fluctuations. Invest with a long term view – five years is a sensible minimum.

When to sell

Selling shares at the right time is almost more important than choosing which ones to buy. Never mind paper profits. The only profits which matter are the ones you take, the money you put in the bank.

The basic rule is to let profits run, and to cut losses quickly. In practice, it seems, private investors often do exactly the opposite. It is easy to persuade yourself that duds need more time, and will come right. And if you take the profit on that winner, you can afford to hang on to the loser a little longer. Do not do it. In practice, someone in the market always knows more than you. Listen to what the share price is telling you. A little dip may not matter. But a consistent fall tells you that other people are selling. They probably have a good reason for it. Try to find out what the reason is by looking in the financial press or asking your broker. Then if you feel it is appropriate, sell your shares.

It is important not to panic and sell whenever a share price falls. Only the most active investors with the time and expertise to follow the stockmarket constantly should be buying and selling on a regular basis. If your hold a well researched, solid and balanced portfolio of investments, a fall in the value of one of your shares should be offset by your other investments and it should be possible to hold for the longer term.

Stop-loss system

Some people, particularly more active investors, swear by a stop-loss system. When you buy a share, you make a mental note to sell should the price fall by more than, say, 20% of the purchase price. Assume that you have bought shares for 100 pence (£1). If the share price fell below 80p, you would automatically sell your shares. Stop loss limits should not be adjusted as share prices fall or they will be ineffective. It takes discipline to stick rigidly to a stop-loss system, and sometimes losers bounce back, and you end up selling a good share. But, in general, a stop-loss is sensible. It means you never lose more than about 20%, plus dealings costs, on any one share.

Running your profits

If you pick a winner, stay with it while it keeps going up. Others are buying it because they think it is good. Perhaps they know more than you. Once shares start moving, they tend to develop a momentum. Success generates success. Fast risers attract attention, and more buyers come in.

You can use a stop-loss system with winners, too. Trail the stop-loss level up behind the share price as it rises. If it slips more than, say, 20% from the peak, take the profits. In other words if the share price moves up from a purchase price of 100p to 200p, you would sell if the share price fell to 160p (200p less 20%). This is known as a rolling stop loss. You never get out at the top that way – only luck can ensure you do that – but you never let big profits slip completely away.

Others advocate selling half of your holding in any share when it doubles, so that the shares you keep have effectively cost you nothing. That works for some, but it takes skill and good fortune to buy a winner. It seems a shame to cut half of your possible gain as it might really be getting going.

It is important to have a system and impose self discipline when it comes to selling shares. Otherwise you will let your portfolio drift, and find yourself holding the duds and selling the good shares.

Timing

You should also try to remember there are times when the going will not be so good. You do not have to be an economic genius to sense when things are getting tougher. The stockmarket is usually among the first indicators. When interest rates are rising and perhaps the pound is under pressure, you know life is going to become more difficult for companies and, subsequently, the stockmarket. A falling or 'bear' market can create panic amongst small investors who rush to sell their holdings before share prices fall further. However, this is often the worst thing to do and here are some points to remember:

- Historically, falls in share prices, even significant falls caused by stockmarket crashes, even out over time. For example, the FTSE All Share Index was back to the level it had reached before the crash of October 1987 within two years and had more than doubled its pre-crash value within 10 years*.

- Good and well researched investment decisions should withstand a bear market (a falling market) as well as a bull market (a rising market). Remember that share prices are falling due to a lack of confidence in the market as a whole and not because of inherent problems with the company in which you have invested.

- Losses on paper do not become real until you sell your shares. Therefore it is best not to sell shares when markets are low unless you have to for a specific purpose. If you hang on, past experience shows that the market is likely to recover and you will be able to sell your shares at a better price in the future.

* Source CSO Finstats

- Panic selling has a cumulative effect and can quicken the downwards trend of a falling market. If you, and other investors like you, hold tight, then the worse excesses of a stockmarket crash can be avoided.

Many of the points that have been made previously about reducing the risk of stockmarket investment apply particularly in a falling market, where it is very important to have a long-term perspective and a balanced portfolio. You might like to adopt a drip feed approach to investment, known as 'pound cost averaging', putting a little money in the stockmarket at regular intervals. This means that you will be buying shares at different times and at different prices, sometimes high and sometimes low, but overall you will pay a price somewhere in the middle, and avoid investing a lump sum at the top of the market. Investing in unit and investment trust saving schemes and participating in an investment club are easy ways to adopt this approach. Chapter Sixteen is dedicated to investment clubs and their benefits.

Many more experienced investors view a falling market as an opportunity to purchase what are fundamentally good investments at a bargain price. ProShare supplies a free *Investor Update* number 12 entitled 'What to do when the market falls', further details of which are contained in Chapter Seventeen.

FIFTEEN

INVESTOR PROTECTION

The single most important phrase for any investor to understand is 'Caveat Emptor' – 'Buyer Beware'. No one cares, or can care, quite as much about what happens to your hard-won cash as you do. This is not a cynical point of view. It is a statement of fact. In many ways, it is a reason for writing this book – a simple practical guide to the investment world that, hopefully, explains the basics.

Knowledge and understanding is, and should be, everyone's best protection against being misled, cheated, or simply being given bad advice.

When it comes to money, ignorance is certainly not bliss. It is irresponsibility. This is not to say that sensible people do not fall victim of fraud – the Maxwell pensioners and the Barlow Clowes investors were truly victims. It is just that when you hand over your money, or take advice, you must be as certain as you can be about the credentials and competence of the people or institutions who are giving it.

There is a mass of legislation, principally in the Financial Services Act (FSA) 1986, designed to prevent fraud and ensure certain standards of professional behaviour by those who handle money on behalf of the investing public. It is important to know your rights – and how to complain when things go wrong. But, equally, you should bear in mind that no system can, or ever will, completely eradicate the possibility of abuse. Your best safeguard is your own common sense, bolstered by real interest in what is happening to your money. You owe it to yourself to think clearly, ask questions and be a little sceptical. That way you will avoid being disappointed – or diddled.

Here are some basic do's and don'ts:

- Don't make investments as a result of a 'cold call'. If a salesman phones you up or arrives at your front door without an appointment, just accept the literature and say you'll get back to them if you are interested. If you have signed on the dotted line, with some investments you are entitled to a two-week 'cooling-off' period during which you may change your mind and get your money back.

- Don't invest in anything that promises unusually high returns for low or no risk. There is usually a catch. If it looks too good to be true, it probably is.

- Don't invest in anything you don't understand. Many people fail to ask basic questions because they think it makes them look ignorant. That gives unscrupulous sales people the chance to baffle them.

- Be careful when dealing with firms or individuals who contact you from overseas. If things go wrong, the likelihood is that you won't be protected by UK legislation.

- Do check the credentials of everyone you deal with, even if they have been recommended by friends or family.

- Do read the small print always.

- Do make sure cheques and deposits are made out to the institution whose investment products you are buying rather than to the intermediary, unless he can show he is authorised to accept your cash.

- Do keep all records of transactions and agreements carefully. That will help avoid misunderstanding and be useful if you have to make a complaint.

- Do make sure you know whether the person giving you financial advice is genuinely independent – or whether you are 'tied' to one particular company. You have a legal right to know.

These common-sense suggestions should mean you avoid most potential pitfalls. There is a regulatory system designed to protect investors. The Financial Services Authority (FSA) is the main watchdog overseeing the self regulating organisations (SROs) that cover key parts of the investment industry. These bodies will all be merged to become part of the single regulator, the FSA (in 1999 by current estimates), but during the transitional phase they will continue with their responsibilities. The SROs authorise firms or individuals to carry on business, impose standards for professional behaviour and competence, make regular checks on their members and will intervene if there is a dispute between a member firm and a customer.

The main SROs are:

- The Investment Management Regulatory Organisation (IMRO), which regulates investment managers. Tel 0171 390 5000.

- The Personal Investment Authority (PIA), which regulates independent financial advisers and those who give advice to investors. Tel 0171 538 8860.

- The Securities and Futures Authority (SFA), which regulates stockbrokers. Tel 0171 378 9000.

In addition, there are nine recognised professional bodies (RPBs) covering solicitors, chartered accountants, insurance brokers, and actuaries which give personal finance advice. The responsibility for the authorisation of members of these professions will also become the responsibility of FSA.

Meanwhile, the crucial point is to check that any firm or individual you deal with is properly authorised. Otherwise, you will not be legally protected in the event of things going wrong. The quickest way to do this is to contact FSA's central register by phoning 0171 929 3652. You can check basic information on particular firms and individuals with them, free of charge.

Investors' Compensation Scheme

However careful you are, things can go wrong. Investment firms can go bust, mishandle clients' money or give negligent advice that results in loss. If any of these things happen, you may have a claim for compensation under the Financial Services Act, provided the firm you dealt with was authorised. If your claim is successful, you will receive a maximum of £48,000 – the first £30,000 in full plus 90% of the next £20,000. It is important to understand the limitations of the compensation scheme – and the fact that it does not cover investment losses due to a fall in the stockmarket. Telephone 0191 628 8820 for details.

When you choose a stockbroker, one of the things you might ask is if the firm has its own insurance to protect clients over and above the level provided by the ICS. If you have a complaint that you can't resolve with your stockbroker, there is a complaints and arbitration procedure. Telephone the SFA on 0171 378 9000.

FSA produces a number of free brochures explaining the system of investor protection and helpful advice on what you should look out for. You can obtain these by telephoning 0171 638 1240.

Investors with access to the internet should look at the FSA website, which includes a useful section on current investment 'scams'. The address is **www.fsa.gov.uk**.

SIXTEEN

INVESTMENT CLUBS

Investing in the stockmarket is not just a way of building up capital or saving for your old age. As any keen investor will tell you, following the stockmarket is a fascinating business. Picking your shares, watching what happens to them, weighing up the economic news, learning to sniff out opportunities, looking out for problems – all these elements mean investors find the stockmarket a stimulating hobby. It can be made even more exciting when they can share their knowledge with others through an investment club.

Investment clubs are not a new idea. There are over 2000 of them up and down the country and thousands more in other countries like the US and France, where investors have found that clubbing together to invest in the stockmarket is profitable and fun.

ProShare believes that investment clubs are one of the most important ways of encouraging individuals to invest in the stockmarket and is actively promoting their formation. ProShare has produced a detailed guide to setting up and running an investment club. If you are the sort of person who enjoys swapping ideas and knowledge, you should consider starting one of your own with like-minded friends.

There are a host of advantages in pooling your stockmarket investments in this way. It can be expensive running your own portfolio, particularly if you only have a modest sum to invest. As we have seen, successful investment involves spreading the risk through buying a number of different shares in a variety of sectors. You may be able to achieve this better, at lower cost, by pooling your resources with others through an investment club. It's like having your own unit trust. And with more money to invest, a club may find it easier to get good advice from the professionals.

Doing your research is a crucial part of successful stockmarket investment. But it is time consuming. Club members can spread the load by agreeing to look at different companies and sectors, maybe specialising in industries where they have particular knowledge or contacts. An investment club is the ideal forum for debating investment ideas. Everyone has their own point of view and discussion is a good way to learn more. Many clubs invite guest speakers to talk about aspects of investment. If you're an absolute beginner, you will learn from other members. If you are an experienced stockmarket investor, it's an opportunity to get together with others who share the same interests.

Members agree how much money each should put in the 'pot', which is usually an initial amount, followed by a set sum each month. So, joining an investment club means that you are setting aside a regular sum for your stockmarket investment. This is a good savings discipline.

The most successful investment clubs work on the basis of co-operation between friends who enjoy meeting each other. You can have your monthly meetings anywhere – at members' houses or in the pub. It should be a sociable event.

There are legal and tax reasons why it is better to limit the number of people in an investment club to 20. Between 10 and 15 is a sensible number to aim for with this many members. There will be enough of you to get the benefits of 'collective' investment, but not to spoil the club atmosphere or make decision-making difficult.

How an investment club works

There are no hard and fast rules about how to organise your investment club, but ProShare has some recommendations on the best way forward. Most important is establishing how the members' investments will be accounted for so that everyone knows how well they are doing.

Typically, the members will put in a lump sum to start with – £50 or £100, or even more depending how quickly you want to start investing. Then the members will fix the regular payment – £15, £20 or more (the amounts can vary between members) that they will make each month. It is important that everyone is comfortable with the amounts chosen. You will probably be wise to wait a couple of months before investing any money – until you have built up a reasonable sum – say £500 minimum. By then you will be really keen to get going with your ideas.

There are different ways of running the fund. ProShare favours the unit valuation system, one of the simplest methods of monitoring the value of members' investments.

At the beginning, each £1 contributed gives members one unit. To work out the value of the units once the fund starts investing, you divide the number of units into the value of the club's assets. Those assets will be cash subscribed, plus the market value of all investments made, minus dealing costs and any other expenses. The fund should be revalued each month. The new unit value is used to calculate the number of units to be purchased with each month's cash subscriptions. Within this framework it is possible for new members to join and for others to buy extra units or, if necessary, sell part of their holding.

Starting an investment club requires careful preparatory work. Getting founding members together is only the first stage. You must then decide who is to chair meetings, who is to look after the administration, where the money will be held, who will have access to it, and what kind of stockmarket dealing or advice service you require.

There may be trustees to be appointed tax implications to be studied and accounting methods to be chosen.

You may find all this a little daunting, which is one reason why ProShare has developed a package of information and support systems to help you and your friends get an investment club up and running.

The ProShare Investment Clubs (PIC) Manual usually costs £25, but is available to readers of *The Investors' Handbook* for £17 plus £3 p&p. At the time of writing, the price of the manual also includes a first year's free membership to PIC, which entitles the club to a regular magazine for each of its club members, a free sample copy of *Company REFS*, access to the PIC help-line and entry into various competitions. To order a copy of the manual by credit card please telephone **0171 394 5200** or write to the following address enclosing a cheque for £20 made payable to ProShare (UK) Limited:

ProShare Investment Clubs
Library Chambers
13 & 14 Basinghall Street
London EC2V 5BQ

SEVENTEEN

PROSHARE

Over the last few years, millions of investors have been introduced to the stockmarket. People who had never owned shares before found it was easy, inexpensive and profitable to invest as the huge formerly State-owned utilities like British Telecom and the gas and electricity industries were transformed into major commercial organisations. Millions of other savers have become shareholders for the first time as their building societies turned themselves into banks and floated on the stockmarket.

But this is just the first step. To many the stockmarket still seems like a baffling and rather frightening place. Where do you go for advice and help? What does all the jargon mean? How can the ordinary investor ever keep up with the professionals? The mystique surrounding the stockmarket is one of the main reasons why relatively few of those who have bought privatisation shares have gone on to invest in others.

To address these problems, ProShare was founded in 1992 as an independent, non-profit-making company with cross party support and funding from HM Treasury, the London Stock Exchange and 22 companies. It is now funded by charitable donations from more than 100 sponsor companies and by grants from the London Stock Exchange, the Gatsby Trust and Sir John Templeton. ProShare's purpose is to promote responsible share based investment, including employee share ownership, through education and research.

One of the main challenges for ProShare has been to ensure that potential and existing shareholders have access to unbiased information about the stockmarket. ProShare does this through an extensive education programme and the provision of user-friendly guidance on investment.

This book, for instance, aims to help the first-time stockmarket investor, while other ProShare publications cater for a variety of needs and includes products both for beginners and the more experienced investor. ProShare lobbies government and the relevant industry bodies to ensure that individual investment operates in a suitable tax and regulatory framework. It helps companies who want to establish employee shareholder schemes and runs ProShare Investment Clubs, which were discussed in the previous chapter. ProShare's products and services available at the time of writing are as follows:

Introduction to Annual Reports and Accounts (£4.95 inc. p&p)

A simple guide to the main features in a company's annual report and accounts, including details on what to look for and how to interpret the information.

The Investor's Guide to Information Sources
(£5.95 inc. p&p)
This guide aims to take the effort out of tracking down useful sources of investment information. These sources range from the simplest, cheapest forms of information, such as daily newspapers to reference publications and internet sites. Also included is a summary of the contents, a rating system and a ProShare comment on each information source.

Portfolio Management System
(£4.95 inc. p&p)
A indispensable paper-based system to enable you to keep track of your investments and account to the Inland Revenue.

Guide to Brokers' New Issues Services
(FREE but please send an A4 size stamped addressed envelope with 39p postage attached if you are not ordering any other products)
A useful guide to the services offered by retail stockbrokers for individuals who wish to gain access to the shares of companies floating on the stockmarket for the first time.

ProShare
Library Chambers
13 & 14 Basinghall Street
London EC2V 5BQ

Or order by credit card by telephoning 0171 394 5200.

ProShare Investor Updates

A series of free fact sheets for individual investors which support ProShare's mission to make investing in shares more accessible to more people. Some of the fact sheets cover basic subjects such as the advantages of stockmarket investment and the things to think about before you invest. Others, pointing out useful sources of stockmarket information and the different taxes that may be incurred when buying and selling shares, are relevant for new and experienced investors alike.

1. *Investing in the stockmarket.* – Covering the potential benefits to be gained from investing in the stockmarket and the things to consider before you start, this Update is ideal for anyone considering investment for the first time.

2. *Choosing the right investment for you* – This covers the relationship between risk and reward, the different circumstances that will affect your choice of investment and offers some golden rules for beginners.

3. *Where to go to get investment advice* – This Update gives information on who to go to for advice on investing in company shares, investment trusts, unit trusts and PEPs.

4. *How to invest* – This Update explains the mechanics of investing and covers the different types of services available when investing in shares, collective investments, gilts and PEPs.

5. *Where to get share information* – Useful for new and experienced investors alike, this Update provides invaluable information on many sources of stockmarket information available from newspapers to on-line services.

6. *Shareholders rights* – A simple guide to your entitlements as a shareholder in a company, covering voting, company literature and dividend payments.

7. *Taxes on share ownership* – This Update gives details on the taxes you have to pay when buying and selling shares and on the income from them.

8. *What is a nominee?* – This explains the implications of holding your shares in a nominee account, the questions you should ask your broker when considering a nominee and the protection of assets. ProShare's Nominee Code is also explained.

9. *RPI figures for Capital Gains Tax calculations* – Giving the retail price index figures since indexation effectively begins, this Update is invaluable a source of the indexation figures you will need when calculating CGT.

10. *CREST and the private investor* – This update explains the implications of the electronic system for transferring UK shares from seller to buyer. It explains the options available to individual investors under CREST.

11. *What is order driven trading?* – This explains the trading system introduced by the London Stock Exchange on 20 October 1997. It looks at how the new system works, and its implications for individual investors, and incorporates a guide to jargon.

12. *What to do when the market falls* – Practical tactics to use in a falling market, some opportunities and stop loss systems.

FREE. For a list of the titles please send a stamped, self addressed envelope with first class postage attached to:

ProShare Investor Update Index
Library Chambers
13 & 14 Basinghall Street
London EC2V 5BQ

If you have access to the Internet, ProShare has a web site including the latest ProShare news and views, the Investor Update series, information on ProShare Investment Clubs and ProShare products and services. The address is **www.proshare.org.uk**.

APPENDIX

A TO Z OF INVESTMENT.

A **AGGREGATE DEMAND** The total demand in the economy for all goods and services.

AIM Alternative Investment Market.

ASSETS What a company owns – land, machinery stocks, cash and investments. Deduct liabilities, like loans and creditors, and you get NET ASSET VALUE – what the company might be worth if it were wound up.

AT BEST An instruction to your stockbroker to buy or sell shares for the best price available.

AUDIT A professional, independent examination of the accounts of a company.

B **BALANCE SHEET** A statement of the assets and liabilities of a company at the end of its financial year.

BEAR MARKET A market which is moving downwards.

BED AND BREAKFAST Selling shares and then buying them back again the next day to reduce the impact of Capital Gains Tax.

BID PRICE The price at which you sell shares.

BIG BANG The day of sweeping changes in the securities industry: 27 October 1986.

BLUE CHIP A big, well-known company whose shares are considered low risk.

BOND A debt where the issuer pays a fixed rate of interest per year and which repays the principal amount on a stated maturity date.

BULL MARKET A rising market.

C

CALL OPTION The right, but not the obligation, to buy stock or shares at an agreed price up to a date in the future.

CAPITAL An investor's savings and wealth, or a company's share capital and reserves.

CAPITAL GAINS TAX A tax on the increase in value of assets sold in a particular year.

COMMISSION The fee that a broker may charge clients for dealing on their behalf.

CONVERTIBLE LOAN STOCKS Securities which pay fixed interest, but can be converted into shares at a given price at set times.

CUM If a share is quoted CUM dividend or CUM rights issue, it means that it still bears the entitlement and this is reflected in the price. CUM is Latin for with.

CREST The UK settlement system for shares.

D **DEPRECIATION** The financial equivalent of wear and tear. Businesses deduct a certain amount for depreciation from profits to reflect the decline in value of plant and machinery.

DEREGULATION Attempting to make a market more efficient by removing or reducing restrictions.

DISCRETIONARY ACCOUNT Your stockbroker or financial adviser can make investment decisions without necessarily consulting you.

DIVIDEND The part of a company's profit (after tax) set aside to pay shareholders.

E **EARNINGS PER SHARE** The amount of profit that can be assigned to each share.

EQUITIES Another term for ordinary shares – the risk-sharing part of a company.

EX A share price may be quoted as EX dividend or EX rights. It means the buyer will not have entitlement to the recent dividend payment or rights issue.

F **FLAT YIELD** The income return on a fixed-interest investment calculated using its current price.

FLOTATION When a company's shares are brought to the stockmarket and quoted for the first time.

FTSE 100 INDEX *The Financial Times* Stock Exchange Index 100; offers up-to-the-minute indications of market performance; sometimes called 'The Footsie'.

G **GEARING** Company borrowing as a proportion of shareholders' funds. A highly geared company is usually seen as a riskier investment.

GILT/GILT EDGED Securities issued by the Government.

GOODWILL Intangible assets, such as reputation.

GROSS Value before deductions. An investment may be described as yielding 10% gross. That means before deduction of income tax.

H **HEDGE** An investment that gives protection – against risk, inflation or exchange rate movements.

I **INDEX-LINKED** The value or return from an investment is tied to the rate of price inflation.

INFLATION A persistent and appreciable increase in the general level of prices; also a fall in the value of money.

INSIDER DEALING Buying or selling of shares by directors, stockbrokers, or others close to the company on the basis of confidential information. This is a criminal offence.

ISSUE PRICE Price at which shares are first offered to investors when a company floats on the stockmarket.

INTERIM DIVIDEND A dividend declared part way through a company's financial year.

INVESTMENT TRUST A company investing in the equity of other companies; investment trust shares are quoted on the Stock Exchange.

L **LIABILITIES** Financial obligations of a company.

LIQUIDITY How easily a company or individual can turn assets into cash (without loss of value).

LIQUIDITY. The value of liquid assets compared with current liabilities.

LISTING The process of having shares quoted in the London Stock Exchange.

LONGS Market term for government stocks (gilts) that have over 15 years to go until they are due to be repaid.

M **MARKET MAKER** A stockmarket trader who offers to buy and sell shares and bonds at all times.

MEDIUMS Market term for gilts (government securities) that have between five and 15 years to go before repayment.

MIDDLE MARKET PRICE Halfway between the buying and selling prices of a share. Most newspapers use the middle market price in their daily stockmarket lists for convenience.

N

NET After deductions. A net return on an investment describes its value after tax has been deducted.

NET ASSET VALUE The net assets of a company divided by the number of shares it has issued.

NEW ISSUE A company coming to the market for the first time or issuing extra shares.

NOMINAL VALUE means the face or par value of shares or other investments as opposed to their market value.

NOMINEE A person or firm holding shares on behalf of another.

O

OFFER FOR SALE A method of bringing a company to the stockmarket. The public can apply for shares directly at a fixed price. A prospectus containing details of the sale must be printed in a national newspaper.

OFFER PRICE Price at which you buy a share.

ORDINARY SHARES Shares where the dividend varies with company profits.

OVERSUBSCRIBED A new issue which attracts more applications than there are shares available.

P

PAR Nominal price of a share or bond as stated on its certificate; it may have no relation to the market value.

PENNY SHARES Shares in companies that are at a very low price.

PORTFOLIO A collection of securities owned by an investor.

PREFERENCE SHARES Securities which rank before ordinary shares for dividend payments, and in the event of a company being wound up, get repaid before equity holders get anything. Preference shares offer a fixed return – the dividends on ordinary shares go up and down depending on profits.

PRICE/EARNINGS RATIO The ratio between share price and earnings per share; sometimes called the 'p/e ratio'.

PREMIUM Upward difference between issue price of a share or other investment and its market value.

PROFIT AND LOSS ACCOUNT Statement detailing revenue and costs, profits (or losses) of a company.

PROSPECTUS A document containing relevant information about a company and a planned share issue. This is a necessary legal requirement for any company issuing shares to the public.

Q **QUOTE** The current price for buying and selling a share offered by a market maker.

R **RIGHTS ISSUE** An invitation to existing shareholders to purchase additional shares in the company.

ROLLING SETTLEMENT A system in which shares have to be paid for within a specific number of days following each transaction.

S **SEAQ** The Stock Exchange Automated Quotation System; a database of share prices which is continually updated.

SECONDARY MARKET Market place for trading in securities that are not new issues.

SETS The Stock Exchange Electronic Trading Service. The 'order driven' system used in the UK for trading in shares in larger companies.

SETTLEMENT When a Stock Exchange transaction is paid for.

SHORTS Market term for gilts (government securities) that have less than five years to go before repayment.

SPREAD The difference between the market-maker's bid and offer prices for a share.

STAG One who buys securities new on the market (new issues) in the hope of selling them quickly for a higher price.

STOCK Any fixed interest security.

STOCKBROKER Someone who buys and sells shares and other Stock Exchange securities on behalf of clients.

SUSPENSION A halt in trading in a share on the Stock Exchange. A company might ask for a temporary suspension of dealings – if a take-over bid is under discussion, for example. Sometimes a suspension means bad news is on the way.

T **TENDER** A way of auctioning shares or gilt-edged securities to the highest bidders. A guide price is announced, then investors have to make up their own minds how much to offer for the number of shares or gilts they want.

TOUCH Competing market makers quote slightly different prices for a share. The touch is the difference between the best bid price and the lowest offer price.

TRANCHE When some part of an issue comes to the market at a different time and possibly at a different price.

TURNOVER Volume of business over a period of time.

U

UNDERWRITE To agree to buy securities that may be left unsold after a new issue. Institutions underwriting an issue will receive a fee for accepting these gilts or bonds which have risk.

UNDATED SECURITIES have no repayment date.

UNIT TRUSTS Collective savings schemes run by specialists which invest in securities.

W

WARRANTS A certificate that gives the holder the right to buy shares at a given price and date.

WORKING CAPITAL Cash and other liquid assets needed to finance the everyday running of a business such as the payment of salaries and the purchase of raw materials. Most companies that go bust do so because a shortage of working capital leads to a cash flow crisis.

Y **YIELD** The annual rate you get on an investment through payment of dividends or interest.

Z **ZERO-COUPON BONDS** Securities which do not pay interest. They are issued at a deep discount to the redemption price so that the investor receives the return in the form of capital gain rather than income.

INDEX